J
342.73   The Bill of Rights
BIL   WITHDRAWN

The Bill of Rights

Gary Zacharias and
Jared Zacharias, *Book Editors*

Daniel Leone, *President*
Bonnie Szumski, *Publisher*
Scott Barbour, *Managing Editor*

 **AT ISSUE IN HISTORY**

GREENHAVEN
PRESS®

San Diego • Detroit • New York • San Francisco • Cleveland
New Haven, Conn. • Waterville, Maine • London • Munich

© 2003 by Greenhaven Press. Greenhaven Press is an imprint of The Gale Group, Inc., a division of Thomson Learning, Inc.

Greenhaven® and Thomson Learning™ are trademarks used herein under license.

For more information, contact
Greenhaven Press
27500 Drake Rd.
Farmington Hills, MI 48331-3535
Or you can visit our Internet site at http://www.gale.com

ALL RIGHTS RESERVED.
No part of this work covered by the copyright hereon may be reproduced or used in any form or by any means—graphic, electronic, or mechanical, including photocopying, recording, taping, Web distribution or information storage retrieval systems—without the written permission of the publisher.

Every effort has been made to trace the owners of copyrighted material.

Cover credit: © Rick Friedman/Black Star Publishing/Picture Quest
Library of Congress, 24, 55
National Archives, 43

LIBRARY OF CONGRESS CATALOGING-IN-PUBLICATION DATA

The Bill of Rights / Gary Zacharias, book editor, Jared Zacharias, book editor.
  p. cm. — (At issue in history)
Includes bibliographical references and index.
ISBN 0-7377-1426-3 (pbk. : alk. paper) — ISBN 0-7377-1425-5 (lib. : alk. paper)
  1. Civil rights—United States—History. 2. Constitutional history—United States. I. Zacharias, Gary. II. Zacharias, Jared. III. Series.
KF4749 .B498 2003
342.73'085—dc21
                                                                2002073857

Printed in the United States of America

Contents

Chapter 2: The Bill of Rights over the Years

Foreword

Historian Robert Weiss defines history simply as "a record and interpretation of past events." Both elements—record and interpretation—are necessary, Weiss argues.

> Names, dates, places, and events are the essence of history. But historical writing is not a compendium of facts. It consists of facts placed in a sequence to tell a connected story. A work of history is not merely a story, however. It also must analyze what happened and *why*—that is, it must interpret the past for the reader.

For example, the events of December 7, 1941, that led President Franklin D. Roosevelt to call it "a date which will live in infamy" are fairly well known and straightforward. A force of Japanese planes and submarines launched a torpedo and bombing attack on American military targets in Pearl Harbor, Hawaii. The surprise assault sank five battleships, disabled or sank fourteen additional ships, and left almost twenty-four hundred American soldiers and sailors dead. On the following day, the United States formally entered World War II when Congress declared war on Japan.

These facts and consequences were almost immediately communicated to the American people who heard reports about Pearl Harbor and President Roosevelt's response on the radio. All realized that this was an important and pivotal event in American and world history. Yet the news from Pearl Harbor raised many unanswered questions. Why did Japan decide to launch such an offensive? Why were the attackers so successful in catching America by surprise? What did the attack reveal about the two nations, their people, and their leadership? What were its causes, and what were its effects? Political leaders, academic historians, and students look to learn the basic facts of historical events and to read the intepretations of these events by many different sources, both primary and secondary, in order to develop a more complete picture of the event in a historical context.

In the case of Pearl Harbor, several important questions surrounding the event remain in dispute, most notably the role of President Roosevelt. Some historians have blamed his policies for deliberately provoking Japan to attack in order to propel America into World War II; a few have gone so far as to accuse him of knowing of the impending attack but not informing others. Other historians, examining the same event, have exonerated the president of such charges, arguing that the historical evidence does not support such a theory.

The Greenhaven At Issue in History series recognizes that many important historical events have been interpreted differently and in some cases remain shrouded in controversy. Each volume features a collection of articles that focus on a topic that has sparked controversy among eyewitnesses, contemporary observers, and historians. An introductory essay sets the stage for each topic by presenting background and context. Several chapters then examine different facets of the subject at hand with readings chosen for their diversity of opinion. Each selection is preceded by a summary of the author's main points and conclusions. A bibliography is included for those students interested in pursuing further research. An annotated table of contents and thorough index help readers to quickly locate material of interest. Taken together, the contents of each of the volumes in the Greenhaven At Issue in History series will help students become more discriminating and thoughtful readers of history.

Introduction

The Bill of Rights—the first ten amendments to the Constitution—guarantees Americans that certain very important freedoms are theirs to keep. Because of the Bill of Rights, the government cannot, for instance, make laws that deny citizens their freedoms of speech, religion, or trial by jury. So vital and integral a part of U.S. law is the Bill of Rights that it is difficult to imagine life without it. Yet as the Constitution was being forged during the summer of 1787, the idea of adding a bill of rights to the document was barely considered.

Almost as an afterthought to the grand work of creating the Constitution, the framers proposed and then rejected a suggestion to include a bill of rights. However, during the process of ratifying the Constitution, it would become apparent, that strong sentiment existed for a bill of rights. Despite the Federalists' contention that state constitutions and, indeed, the proposed Constitution itself guaranteed the people's rights, their opponents were eventually to prevail. Patrick Henry of Virginia, speaking in favor of such a bill, said, "If you intend to reserve your unalienable rights, you must have the most express stipulation."

After the Constitution was ratified, debate continued as to the need for that "express stipulation" of rights. Then, after the issues were discussed and the votes were cast, ten amendments were added to the Constitution. In December 1791 the Bill of Rights became law.

Precedent for a Bill of Rights

Abundant precedent for a bill of rights existed in early English law. As the American colonies grew, the people insisted that they should enjoy all the fundamental rights of Englishmen. They claimed to be beneficiaries of the Magna Carta, signed in 1215, which legally limited the king's power. That document presented a clear statement on due process, meaning that no one could be punished by the government unless certain fair procedures were followed.

In addition, American colonists looked back to later English laws. One such law allowed for the writ of habeas corpus. In 1626 knights who had been imprisoned by the king challenged the legal basis for their incarceration by seeking such a writ, saying the king himself was subject to the law and had to answer to it. Two years later the Petition of Right was passed, which reinforced the idea that the rule of law reigned supreme over even the highest power of the land. It specifically guaranteed that no taxes could be levied without the consent of Parliament and outlawed the unpopular practice of quartering soldiers in private homes.

One other key English document of rights with which American colonists were familiar was the Bill of Rights, which was created after a huge political upheaval in England. In 1688 King James II, a Roman Catholic, wanted to restore Catholicism and absolute monarchy to the nation. Leaders of Parliament balked at this idea and urged two others to rule England: James's daughter, the Protestant Mary, and her husband, William of Orange, ruler of the Netherlands. Later the same year, William landed in England with an army, and James fled. After this Glorious Revolution, as it was called, William and Mary agreed in 1689 to accept Parliament's Bill of Rights. For the first time, *bill of rights* was used as a term of law. It consolidated laws from the past, granting liberties in various areas: It prohibited cruel and unusual punishment and excessive bail, and it provided for the right to bear arms and the right of petition for relief of grievances.

The Influence of John Locke

When the French and Indian Wars ended in 1763, tensions mounted between England and its American colonies that soon led to intense debates over rights. The British had incurred tremendous costs in defeating the French, so Parliament passed laws taxing Americans and restricting their freedoms. The colonists eagerly embraced the essays of the English philosopher John Locke (1632–1704), who had argued that natural laws superceded man-made laws. It was from these natural laws that individuals gained such natural rights as life, liberty, and property. No government should attempt to take those rights away, and individuals should guard against any such government infringement. A government was in place to protect those natural rights, and any time such a government violated its duty, the people had the right to disempower it.

American colonists at that time experienced abuses of governmental power that led them to consider Locke's ringing statement of their right to replace an abusive government. One pivotal event took place in 1765 when the English Parliament passed the Stamp Act. It imposed taxes on all legal and business documents as well as newspapers, books, and pamphlets. This act was enforced through writs of assistance issued by Parliament, by which British customs inspectors entered homes—even if they had no evidence of there having been a Stamp Act violation—and searched through everything in the home, looking for evidence of wrongdoing. Colonists despised these searches conducted without warrants. Americans believed they had to rein in governmental power in order to protect their rights.

In 1776 Thomas Jefferson beautifully captured Locke's ideas of rights in the Declaration of Independence. Jefferson wrote that "governments are instituted among men, deriving their just powers from the consent of the governed. That whenever any form of government becomes destructive of these ends, it is the right of the people to alter or abolish it." Both government and the individual had a job to do: The government promised to protect the individual, and the individual agreed to follow the laws of the government. When the government failed at its job, the people had the right to dissolve their bonds with that government.

State Efforts to Protect Rights

In 1781 Americans established the Articles of Confederation, under which all states would be governed, creating a situation in which rights were in the hands of state governments. Because the delegates who created that document hated the abuses of the British Crown and Parliament, they set up a confederation with an extremely weak national government. The document guaranteed each state's sovereignty and independence. Whatever rights Americans sought were to be found in state documents rather than on the national level. Six states had adopted their own bill of rights based on early English laws. Those states that did not have their own separate bill of rights had incorporated fundamental guarantees into their state constitutions or used the wording in their original colonial charters. For example, Rhode Island had a charter (1663) with a grand statement of religious liberty that was inspired by the state's founder, Roger Williams. In addition, Pennsylvania had set up its own charter in 1701 with phrases such as "enjoyment of civil liberties" and a reference to God as "the only Lord of conscience." The Continental Congress in 1774 had passed a declaration that protested acts of Parliament as being "dangerous and destructive of American rights." This declaration also claimed that Americans had the right to "life, Liberty, and property" which they had not given up to any government. Thomas Jefferson, in addition to writing the Declaration of Independence, also wrote Virginia's Bill for Establishing Religious Freedom, which guaranteed religious liberty and equality. One other document, the Northwest Ordinance of 1787, also promised several basic freedoms for individuals who wished to establish themselves in the wilderness.

The Constitutional Convention

The Constitutional Convention, which met all through the summer of 1787, produced a document that surprisingly did not include a bill of rights. Just five days before the convention adjourned, two members asked for the inclusion of a bill of rights to serve as a preface to the Constitution. But the motion was shortly rejected without receiving the vote of a single state. This was undoubtedly the most serious miscalculation the delegates made because it was later to play a large role in debates over the ratification of the Constitution.

James Madison, rightly regarded as "the Father of the Constitution," had been concerned with issues of rights for nearly his entire life. For example, he secured an amendment to the Virginia Declaration of Rights of 1776 that granted all men free exercise of religion. During the mid-1780s he secured passage of the Bill for Religious Freedom that Jefferson had originally drafted for Virginia in 1779; this bill has been regarded as a landmark in the struggle for religious liberty.

However, Madison began to change his thinking regarding rights soon after passage of this bill. He reached the conclusion that the people themselves, acting through their representatives, were the chief threat to rights and that any formal declaration of rights would not necessarily restrain any legislature. Madison came to doubt the value of bills of rights not because it was too hard to draw up a list of agreed-upon rights but because majorities could ignore these rights and enact unjust laws. He, as well as most of the other delegates to the Constitutional Convention, saw little evidence that state declarations of rights had helped secure their objectives. Instead of drawing up a separate bill of rights, the delegates inserted several rights within the proposed Constitution, such as trial by jury in criminal cases and the writ of habeas corpus.

When the states met to debate ratification of the Constitution, those in favor of its adoption, the Federalists, soon learned that the omission of a bill of rights would cause them many problems. For example, Richard Henry Lee indicated the general concerns that anti-Federalists shared when he detailed specific rights that needed explicit protection: freedom of the press, prohibitions on excessive bail and cruel and unusual punishment, the right to petition, free elections, and trial by jury. Federalists hit back by claiming that some rights were already included in the Constitution. But anti-Federalists asked why some rights were included while other rights were not. Those opposed to the Constitution voiced their suspicion that Congress would have too much power. They also argued that a bill of rights was needed to act as a yardstick for the people to measure whether their leaders were violating their rights. Anti-Federalists suggested that traditional rights and liberties would be rendered insecure if they went undeclared. The Federalist response was that it was too difficult to create a single list because some rights might be inadvertently left off, possibly causing people to believe that they were not entitled to those rights. In addition, they echoed Madison's complaint that bills of rights were easily ignored by political majorities. During the debates over ratification, Federalists did offer a concession that a bill of rights would be added later to the Constitution.

When Congress met in 1789 for its first session after ratification of the Constitution, it was James Madison, surprisingly, who led the way for an addition of a bill of rights. He had by now decided that a bill of rights would be helpful for several reasons: It would educate the public on the fundamentals of free government; it would bring the dissenting states of North Carolina and Rhode Island back into the union; it would redeem a campaign promise made by Federalists; and it would counteract illegal acts of the government. In addition, he was concerned because there were calls from anti-Federalists for a second convention, which could be a political nightmare. After much debate and squabbling, a list of proposed amendments was ready by the end of September. When 1791 ended, enough states had ratified ten of the amendments to make them part of the Constitution.

The story of the Bill of Rights after ratification is one of irony. Despite the huge uproar over ratification, the document soon dropped from the focus of national politics. Other issues came to the forefront, such as choosing the location of the capital of the United States, deciding how to handle federal debts, creating a bank of the United States, and analyzing the French Revolution's impact on American politics. In the federal system created under the new Constitution, the states had constitutional power to regulate the sphere of civil liberty. In a decentralized constitutional system, liberty was primarily corporate and local in nature.

It took major upheavals and the passage of a great deal of time before civil liberties and civil rights evolved into what we know them to be today. Prior to the Civil War, despite the existence of the Bill of Rights, individual states were able to set limits on individual rights. The Civil War brought about the passage of the Fourteenth Amendment, which barred states from denying people their due process or equal protection of law. Decades later, in the mid-twentieth century, courts began using those terms to protect individual rights from state infringement. The history of the 1900s reveals the continuing efforts of federal courts to expand the rights guaranteed to every person.

Today the Bill of Rights plays a vital role in the struggle of people who seek to gain or retain their share of the American dream. Sometimes that role may seem conflicted. For instance, not infrequently one person's rights may seem to infringe on the rights of another person, and the matter must then be decided in a courtroom. In other cases citizens who claim their rights have been violated file lawsuits that may be frivolous in nature. Such lawsuits can clog court dockets and slow the course of justice for cases that have true merit. However, although the role of the Bill of Rights in society may appear to have changed over time, its mission remains essentially the same as when James Madison wrote it: to enumerate and to guarantee protection of the rights and liberties of the people.

Chapter 1

Early Debates over the Bill of Rights

1

The Constitutional Convention Rejects a Bill of Rights

Catherine Drinker Bowen

Catherine Drinker Bowen is a historian and a biographer of Francis Bacon, Edward Coke, John Adams, Oliver Wendell Holmes, and others. In the selection below, Bowen discusses the last few days of the Constitutional Convention when the delegates voted down the inclusion of a bill of rights. Most of the delegates believed the proposed Constitution was restrictive enough in its powers and thus did not need an additional enumeration of rights. They saw the Constitution as a bill of rights itself, made for a free people. Others, however, criticized the delegates for failing to include a bill of rights in the Constitution.

"We hear," said the *Pennsylvania Packet* on September sixth, [1787,] "that the Convention propose to adjourn next week." Exultantly pro-Constitutional, the *Packet* let fly in its best style: "The year 1776 is celebrated for a revolution in favor of Liberty. The year 1787 it is expected will be celebrated with equal joy, for a revolution in favor of Government." Later the *Packet* gave space to a "paragraph writer"—current name for columnist—who let himself imagine that the Constitution had been rejected by the states. He described the nation's plight: "His Excellency Daniel Shays has taken possession of the Massachusetts government and the former encumbents are to be executed

Excerpted from *Miracle at Philadelphia*, by Catherine Drinker Bowen (New York: Little, Brown and Company, 1966). Copyright © 1966 by Little, Brown and Company. Reprinted with permission.

tomorrow. New Jersey has petitioned to be taken again under the protection of the British Crown. . . ."

On September twelfth, Dr. [William Samuel] Johnson [of the Connecticut delegation] noted in his diary that it was very hot; for the most part the weather had been blessedly cool while the Committee of Style did its work. That morning, a Wednesday, the committee presented their Constitution; Johnson referred to it in the now customary phrase as "the plan." The Convention, unimpressed, or conscious perhaps that this was their last chance, proceeded to tear the plan apart as they had done with every previous version since May. . . . Let the President's negative be overruled only by two-thirds of Congress, not three-fourths. . . . Include a provision for jury trials in civil cases. . . . The first motion won by close vote, the second hung fire; [Elbridge] Gerry proposed that the Committee of Style provide such a clause for consideration.

Bill of Rights Idea Dismissed

Trial by jury had long been a sacred trinity of words, celebrated as the palladium of liberty and accompanied by panegyric about the rights of man and the ancient privileges come down from our Saxon ancestors. Actually, trial by jury had by no means insured fair treatment in court these many centuries; time was, in England, when juries were easily intimidated by judge or lordly defendant. Nevertheless trial by jury was a phrase to conjure with. This morning it inspired [Virginia delegate] George Mason to say the first word of the summer about a bill of rights for the Constitution. He wished, Mason said, "the plan had been prefaced with a bill of rights. It would give great quiet to the people." Such a bill could be prepared in a few hours, Mason added, if the committee simply referred to the various state declarations.

He wished, Mason said, "the plan had been prefaced with a bill of rights. It would give great quiet to the people."

Eight of the state constitutions included bills of rights. Mason himself had written Virginia's in 1776. Elbridge Gerry now moved for the preparation of such a bill and Mason seconded him. Roger Sherman, however, said the state declarations were sufficient; after all, they were not repealed by the new Constitution. Mason said no to this; the laws of the United States were now to be the supreme law of the land and therefore paramount to state bills of rights. Ten states to none, the Convention voted against adding a bill of rights to the Constitution. Massachusetts was absent. Gerry must have left the chamber. Even Virginia voted no.

Thus summarily was the question dismissed, a reaction which at first seems extraordinary. So familiar are Americans today with the Bill of Rights that they confuse it with the first seven articles which in September of 1787 made up the whole body of the Constitution. If challenged, many citizens would say the United States Constitution is that document which begins *We the People* and guarantees freedom of speech and religion, *habeas corpus* [protection against illegal imprisonment] and so on. Actually, of course, the Bill of Rights consists of the first ten amendments to the Constitution, suggested by the states during the ratification period and passed by the first Congress (1789) under the new government.

When the Constitution was published in the newspapers after the Convention rose, and the Antifederalists gathered their strength for opposition, nothing created such an uproar as the lack of a bill of rights. What had the Convention been thinking of, to neglect a matter so elementary, so much a part of the heritage of free people? Why, the business went back to Magna Carta! Blackstone had defined it, and Lord Coke before him in his *Second Institute*.

Why the Bill of Rights Was Rejected

The Convention's stand, however, was reasonable, if mistaken. No delegate had been against such rights. Merely they considered the Constitution covered the matter as it stood. And when, shortly after the ten-to-nothing vote, [Charles] Pinckney and Gerry moved for a declaration "that the liberty of the press should be inviolably observed," Roger Sherman said at once it was unnecessary; the power of Congress did not extend to the press. Seven to four the states again voted no.

There is a fascination in reading the delegates' later defense of their position. To Alexander Hamilton a bill of rights was more than unnecessary. It would be dangerous, he said. "Why declare that things shall not be done which there is no power [in Congress] to do?" Hamilton argued that bills of rights originally were stipulations between kings and their subjects, like Magna Carta, which was "obtained by the barons, sword in hand, from King John." Whereas in the American government the people, having surrendered nothing and retained everything, have no need of particular reservations. *"We the People of the United States . . ."* Hamilton quoted the preamble—a firmer recognition of popular rights, he said, than volumes of those aphorisms appearing in the state bills of rights, which "would sound much better in a treatise of ethics than in a constitution of government." And while at it, why not declare in the Constitution that government ought to be free, that taxes ought not to be excessive, and so on?

As for James Wilson, he told a meeting of Pennsylvania citizens that a bill of rights would not only have been unnecessary but impracticable. "Enumerate all the rights of men? I am sure that no gentleman in the late Convention would have attempted such a thing." The new Constitution in Wilson's view was not a body of fundamental law which would require a statement of natural rights. Rather it was municipal law, positive law—what in medieval days was called jus civile. Not a declaration of eternal rights but a code for reference.

Quite evidently the Federal Convention looked on its work as practical, everyday business; all along they had avoided high-flown phrases about the rights of man. Such rights, John Dickinson was to argue in the newspapers—trial by jury, no taxation without representation—"must be preserved by soundness of sense and honesty of heart." Compared with these qualities, what, he demanded, are bills of rights? "Do we want to be reminded that the sun enlightens, warms, invigorates, and cheers? or how horrid it would be, to have his blessed beams intercepted, by our being thrust into mines or dungeons? Liberty is the sun of society, and Rights are the beams."

Roger Sherman never changed his stand against a bill of rights. In his forthright way he wrote about it to a New Haven paper, signing himself "A Countryman." "No bill of rights," said Sherman, "ever yet bound the supreme power longer than the honeymoon of a new married couple, unless the rulers were interested in preserving the rights; and in that case they have always been ready enough to declare the rights, and to preserve them when they were declared."

Controversy over the Decision

The newspapers were to be flooded with letters and articles on the subject. . . . Noah Webster, stung by the New York convention's arguments for a bill of rights, addressed the members (via the newspapers) in his best free-swinging sarcasm. To complete their list of unalienable rights, Webster suggested a clause "that everybody shall, in good weather, hunt on his own land, and catch fish in rivers that are public property . . . and that Congress shall never restrain any inhabitant of America from eating and drinking, at seasonable times, or prevent his lying on his left side, in a long winter's night, or even on his back, when he is fatigued by lying on his right."

Dr. Benjamin Rush was to tell the Pennsylvania convention for ratification that he "considered it an honor to the late convention that this system has not been disgraced with a bill of rights. Would it not be absurd to frame a formal declaration that our natural rights are acquired from ourselves?" Down in South Carolina, General Charles Cotesworth Pinckney delivered the nakedest statement of all. Bills of rights, he told the legislature, "generally begin with declaring that all men are by nature born free. Now, we should make that declaration with a very bad grace, when a large part of our property consists in men who are actually born slaves."

Such rights should be constantly kept in view, in addresses, in bills of rights, in newspapers, and so on.

Such were the arguments against a bill of rights for the Constitution. The reasons in favor scarcely need quotation; they are part of our thinking today. There were, however, surprising twists to men's expression of their convictions. Jefferson for instance was indignant at the omission of a bill of rights and hoped "Virginia's opposition would remedy this." But, writing to General Washington from Paris, Jefferson classed the omission of a bill of rights as only one of two things that he disliked strongly in the new Constitution.

The other was the perpetual re-eligibility of the President, which he feared would "make that an office for life, first, and then hereditary."

Lesser men had their say; everywhere, people took part. In Portland, Maine, a printer named Thomas Wait, publisher of the *Cumberland Gazette*, maintained "there was a certain darkness, duplicity and studied ambiguity of expression running through the whole Constitution which renders a bill of rights peculiarly necessary. As it now stands, but very few individuals do or ever will understand it, consequently Congress will be its own interpreter."

It was a shrewd and very natural reaction. The Constitution was new and shocking, and minds offended by novelty are apt to complain of darkness or ambiguity in matters not yet digested. Luther Martin in Maryland raised a great outcry, hinting that the lack of a bill of rights was deliberate and scandalous. Oliver Ellsworth replied angrily in the newspapers, signing himself "A Landholder." Why had Mr. Martin never spoken out in the Convention for a bill of rights? "You, sir," wrote Ellsworth, "never signified by any motion or expression whatever, that [the plan] stood in need of a bill of rights, or in any wise endangered the trial by jury. In these respects the Constitution met your entire approbation; for had you believed it defective in these essentials, you ought to have mentioned it in Convention, or had you thought it wanted further guards, it was your indispensable duty to have proposed them." Martin floundered badly in his reply, said that he had indeed prepared and even drafted a bill of rights toward the end of the Convention, but had been advised against presenting it. "Ambition and interest," wrote Martin, had "so far blinded the understanding of some of the principal framers of the Constitution . . . I most sacredly believe their object is the total abolition and destruction of all state governments, and the erection on their ruins of one great and extensive empire. . . ."

With charity and much perceptive good sense, Richard Henry Lee of Virginia, a congressman—no member of the Convention and fiercely anti-Constitutionalist—excused the Convention's fault concerning a bill of rights. Lee said that when men have long and early understood certain matters as the common concerns of the country, they are apt to suppose these things are understood by others and need not be expressed. "And it is not uncommon," Lee added, "for the ablest men frequently to make this mistake. Whereas such rights should be constantly kept in view, in addresses, in bills of rights, in newspapers, and so on."

The Convention records bear Lee out. The framers looked upon the Constitution as a bill of rights in itself; all its provisions were for a free people and a people responsible. Why, therefore, enumerate the things that Congress must not do?

2

Two Founding Fathers Debate the Bill of Rights

Thomas Jefferson and James Madison

It was ironic that a man so closely connected with the founding of the American nation, Thomas Jefferson, was not even in the country when the Constitutional Convention took place. He was in Paris, sent there in 1784 to help John Adams and Benjamin Franklin negotiate European treaties of commerce. He later served as president of the United States from 1801 to 1809. James Madison, only thirty-six years old at the time, represented Virginia at the Constitutional Convention in 1787. Known as the "Father of the Constitution," Madison not only helped create the document, but he also wrote parts of *The Federalist*, a well-respected series of letters to newspapers designed to help ensure that states ratified the Constitution. He was a congressman, secretary of state, and the fourth president of the United States (1809–1817).

The letters below are an exchange of ideas regarding a bill of rights. Jefferson, in his December 1787 letter, discusses what he likes and does not like about the new Constitution; he complains about a lack of a bill of rights in the document. In his letter dated October 17, 1788, Madison lets Jefferson know he is in favor of adding a bill of rights, but he states that he does not consider it essential for several reasons, including his belief that the rights are reserved to the people, that the federal government has been created with limited powers, and that a bill of rights is no guarantee of protection against a determined tyranny. Jefferson's letter of March 1789 is a response to Madison's letter from the previous October. Jefferson adds another reason for including a bill of rights—it would allow the judiciary a legal way to check any repression of rights. In addition, Jefferson attempts to answer Madison's ob-

Excerpted from letters exchanged between Thomas Jefferson and James Madison, by Thomas Jefferson and James Madison, December 1787–March 1789.

jections against the proposed bill. He closes by admitting that a bill of rights may cramp legal activities of the government, but he argues that there will be more difficulties if the country does not have one.

Thomas Jefferson to James Madison, December 20, 1787.

The season admitting only of operations in the Cabinet, and these being in a great measure secret, I have little to fill a letter. I will therefore make up the deficiency by adding a few words on the Constitution proposed by our Convention. I like much the general idea of framing a government which should go on of itself peaceably, without needing continued recurrence to the state legislatures. I like the organization of the government into Legislative, Judiciary and Executive. I like the power given the Legislature to levy taxes; and for that reason solely approve of the greater house being chosen by the people directly. For tho' I think a house chosen by them will be very illy qualified to legislate for the Union, for foreign nations &c. yet this evil does not weigh against the good of preserving inviolate the fundamental principle that the people are not to be taxed but by representatives chosen immediately by themselves. I am captivated by the compromise of the opposite claims of the great and little states, of the latter to equal, and the former to proportional influence. I am much pleased too with the substitution of the method of voting by persons, instead of that of voting by states: and I like the negative given to the Executive with a third of either house, though I should have liked it better had the Judiciary been associated for that purpose, or invested with a similar and separate power. There are other good things of less moment. I will now add what I do not like. First the omission of a bill of rights providing clearly and without the aid of sophisms for freedom of religion, freedom of the press, protection against standing armies, restriction against monopolies, the eternal and unremitting force of the habeas corpus laws, and trials by jury in all matters of fact triable by the laws of the land and not by the law of Nations. To say, as Mr. [James] Wilson does that a bill of rights was not necessary because all is reserved in the case of the general government which is not

given, while in the particular ones all is given which is not
reserved might do for the Audience to whom it was addressed, but is surely gratis dictim [a statement not supported by fact], opposed by strong inferences from the body
of the instrument, as well as from the omission of the clause
of our present confederation which had declared that in express terms. It was a hard conclusion to say because there
has been no uniformity among the states as to the cases triable by jury, because some have been so incautious as to
abandon this mode of trial, therefore the more prudent
states shall be reduced to the same level of calamity. It would
have been much more just and wise to have concluded the
other way that as most of the states had judiciously preserved this palladium, those who had wandered should be
brought back to it, and to have established general right instead of general wrong. Let me add that a bill of rights is
what the people are entitled to against every government on
earth, general or particular, and what no just government
should refuse, or rest on inference. . . .

James Madison to Thomas Jefferson, October 17, 1788.

The little pamphlet herewith inclosed will give you a col-
lective view of the alterations which have been proposed for
the new Constitution. Various and numerous as they appear
they certainly omit many of the true grounds of opposition.
The articles relating to Treaties, to paper money, and to
contracts, created more enemies than all the errors in the
System positive and negative put together. It is true nevertheless that not a few, particularly in Virginia have contended for the proposed alterations from the most honorable and patriotic motives; and that among the advocates for
the Constitution there are some who wish for further
guards to public liberty and individual rights. As far as these
may consist of a constitutional declaration of the most essential rights, it is probable they will be added; though there
are many who think such addition unnecessary, and not a
few who think it misplaced in such a Constitution. There is
scarce any point on which the party in opposition is so much
divided as to its importance and its propriety. My own opinion has always been in favor of a bill of rights; provided it be
so framed as not to imply powers not meant to be included
in the enumeration. At the same time I have never thought

the omission a material defect, nor been anxious to supply it even by subsequent amendment, for any other reason than that it is anxiously desired by others. I have favored it because I supposed it might be of use, and if properly executed could not be of disservice.

Why a Bill of Rights Is Unnecessary

I have not viewed it in an important light 1. Because I conceive that in a certain degree, though not in the extent argued by Mr. Wilson, the rights in question are reserved by the manner in which the federal powers are granted. 2. Because there is great reason to fear that a positive declaration of some of the most essential rights could not be obtained in the requisite latitude. I am sure that the rights of conscience in particular, if submitted to public definition would be narrowed much more than they are likely ever to be by an assumed power. One of the objections in New England was that the Constitution by prohibiting religious tests opened a door for Jews Turks and infidels. 3. Because the limited powers of the federal Government and the jealousy of the subordinate Governments, afford a security which has not existed in the case of the State Governments, and exists in no other. 4. Because experience proves the inefficacy of a bill of

Thomas Jefferson

rights on those occasions when its controul is most needed. Repeated violations of these parchment barriers have been committed by overbearing majorities in every State. In Virginia I have seen the bill of rights violated in every instance where it has been opposed to a popular current. Notwithstanding the explicit provision contained in that instrument for the rights of Conscience it is well known that a religious establishment would have taken place in that State, if the legislative majority had found as they expected, a majority of the people in favor of the measure; and I am persuaded that if a majority of the people were now of one sect, the measure would still take place and on narrower ground than was then proposed, notwithstanding the additional obstacle which the law has since created. Wherever the real power in a Government lies, there is the danger of oppression. In our Governments the real power lies in the majority of the Community, and the invasion of private rights is *chiefly* to be apprehended, not from acts of Government contrary to the sense of its constituents, but from acts in which the Government is the mere instrument of the major number of the constituents. This is a truth of great importance, but not yet sufficiently attended to: and is probably more strongly impressed on my mind by facts, and reflections suggested by them, than on yours which has contemplated abuses of power issuing from a very different quarter. Wherever there is an interest and power to do wrong, wrong will generally be done, and not less readily by a powerful and interested party than by a powerful and interested prince. The difference, so far as it relates to the superiority of republics over monarchies, lies in the less degree of probability that interest may prompt abuses of power in the former than in the latter; and in the security in the former against oppression of more than the smaller part of the Society, whereas in the former it may be extended in a manner to the whole. The difference so far as it relates to the point in question—the efficacy of a bill of rights in controuling abuses of power—lies in this: that in a monarchy the latent force of the nation is superior to that of the Sovereign, and a solemn charter of popular rights must have a great effect, as a standard for trying the validity of public acts, and a signal for rousing and uniting the superior force of the community; whereas in a popular Government, the political and physical power may be considered as vested in the same hands, that is in a majority of the people, and consequently the tyrannical will of the sovereign is not to be controuled by the dread of an appeal to any other force within the community.

Value of a Bill of Rights

What use then it may be asked can a bill of rights serve in popular Governments? I answer the two following which though less essential than in other Governments, sufficiently recommended the precaution. 1. The political truths declared in that solemn manner acquire by degrees the character of fundamental maxims of free Government, and as they become incorporated with the national sentiment, counteract the impulses of interest and passion. 2. Altho' it be generally true as above stated that the danger of oppression lies in the interested majorities of the people rather than in usurped acts of the Government, yet there may be occasions on which the evil may spring from the latter sources; and on such, a bill of rights will be a good ground for an appeal to the sense of the community. Perhaps too there may be a certain degree of danger, that a succession of artful and ambitious rulers, may by gradual and well-timed advances, finally erect an independent Government on the subversion of liberty. Should this danger exist at all, it is prudent to guard against it, especially when the precaution can do no injury. At the same time I must own that I see no tendency in our governments to danger on that side. It has been remarked that there is a tendency in all Governments to an augmentation of power at the expence of liberty. But the remark as usually understood does not appear to me well founded. Power when it has attained a certain degree of energy and independence goes on generally to further degrees of relaxation, until the abuses of liberty beget a sudden transition to an undue degree of power. With this explanation the remark may be true; and in the latter sense only is it in my opinion applicable to the Governments in America. It is a melancholy reflection that liberty should be equally exposed to danger whether the Government have too much or too little power; and that the line which divides these extremes should be so inaccurately defined by experience. . . .

Thomas Jefferson to James Madison, March 15, 1789.

. . . Your thoughts on the subject of the Declaration of rights in the letter of Oct. 17. I have weighed with great satisfaction. Some of them had not occurred to me before, but were acknowledged just in the moment they were presented to my mind. In the arguments in favor of a declaration of rights, you omit one which has great weight with me, the legal check which it puts into the hands of the judiciary. This is a body, which if rendered independent, and kept strictly to their own department merits great confidence for their learning and integrity. In fact what degree of confidence would be too much for a body composed of such men as Wythe, Blair, and Pendleton? On characters like these the "civium ardor prava jubentium" [the evil passion of citizens who give orders] would make no impression. I am happy to find that on the whole you are a friend to this amendment. The Declaration of rights is like all other human blessings alloyed with some inconveniences, and not accomplishing fully its object. But the good in this instance vastly outweighs the evil.

Response to Madison's Objections

I cannot refrain from making short answers to the objections which your letter states to have been raised. 1. That the rights in question are reserved by the manner in which the federal powers are granted. Answer. A constitutive act may certainly be so formed as to need no declaration of rights. The act itself has the force of a declaration as far as it goes: and if it goes to all material points nothing more is wanting. In the draught of a constitution which I had once a thought of proposing in Virginia, and printed afterwards, I endeavored to reach all the great objects of public liberty, and did not mean to add a declaration of rights. Probably the object was imperfectly executed: but the deficiencies would have been supplied by others in the course of discussion. But in a constitutive act which leaves some precious articles unnoticed, and raises implications against others, a declaration of rights becomes necessary by way of supplement. This is the case of our new federal constitution. This instrument forms us into one state as to certain objects, and gives us a legislative and executive body for these objects. It should therefore guard us against their abuses of power within the field submitted to them. 2. A positive declaration of some essential rights could not be obtained in the requisite latitude. Answer. Half a loaf is better than no bread. If we cannot secure all our rights, let us secure what we can. 3. The limited powers of the federal government and jealousy of the subordinate governments afford a security which exists in no other instance. Answer. The first member of this seems resolvable into the 1st objection before stated. The jealousy of the subordinate governments is a precious reliance. But observe that those governments are only agents. They must have principles furnished them whereon to found their opposition. The declaration of rights will be the text whereby they will try all the acts of the federal government. In this view it is necessary to the federal government also: as by the same text they may try the opposition of the subordinate governments. 4. Experience proves the inefficacy of a bill of rights. True. But tho it is not absolutely efficacious under all circumstances, it is of great potency always, and rarely inefficacious. A brace the more will often keep up the building which would have fallen with that brace the less.

Bill of Rights: Problems With and Without

There is a remarkeable difference between the characters of the Inconveniencies which attend a Declaration of rights, and those which attend the want of it. The inconveniencies of the Declaration are that it may cramp government in its useful exertions. But the evil of this is shortlived, moderate, and reparable. The inconveniencies of the want of a Declaration are permanent, afflicting and irreparable: they are in constant progression from bad to worse. The executive in our governments is not the sole, it is scarcely the principal object of my jealousy. The tyranny of the legislatures is the most formidable dread at present, and will be for long years. That of the executive will come in its turn, but it will be at a remote period. I know there are some among us who would now establish a monarchy. But they are inconsiderable in number and weight of character. The rising race are all republicans. We were educated in royalism: no wonder if some of us retain that idolatry still. Our young people are educated in republicanism. An apostacy from that to royalism is unprecedented and impossible. I am much pleased with the prospect that a declaration of rights will be added: and hope it will be done in that way which will not endanger the whole frame of the government, or any essential part of it.

3

Federalists and Anti-Federalists Clash over the Bill of Rights

Jack N. Rakove

Jack N. Rakove, a history professor at Stanford University, has written *The Beginnings of National Politics: An Interpretive History of the Continental Congress* and *James Madison and the Creation of the American Republic.* In the selection below, he summarizes the arguments of Federalists and anti-Federalists in the debate over the need for a bill of rights. Anti-Federalists, who opposed the Constitution, detailed specific rights that needed protection, especially in the administration of justice. They asked why the Constitution included some rights but not others. Patrick Henry, the famous anti-Federalist orator and politician, was suspicious of Congress, claiming it would violate rights without a set list of the people's just claims. Other anti-Federalists argued that a bill of rights provided standards of certainty as a way to assess acts of government. In addition, anti-Federalists believed a written list of rights would once and for all establish clearly the traditional rights they had operated under for so long. On the other hand, an early Federalist, James Wilson, responded that Congress would adopt suitable regulations and that whatever rights were not given specifically to the government via the Constitution were reserved for the people. Rakove explains that the Federalists rejected the inclusion of a list of rights because they believed it would lead to unending nit-picking. They felt liberty was better served by avoiding a list and definition of rights. In addition, they were concerned that any enumeration of rights might accidentally

Excerpted from *Original Meanings*, by Jack N. Rakove (New York: Alfred A. Knopf, 1997). Copyright © 1997 by Jack N. Rakove. Reprinted with permission.

leave one out, causing people to believe that particular right was not given to the people.

Federalists learned early that the omission of a bill of rights would weigh heavily against them. Though [George] Mason made it the first of his objections to the Constitution, Federalists took their earliest alarm from the amendments that Richard Henry Lee proposed when Congress debated how to convey the Constitution to the states, and from the published dissent of the minority assemblymen in Pennsylvania. Both had seen Mason's objections before they acted, but while the assemblymen simply restated his points as rhetorical questions, Lee better indicated the general concerns that Anti-Federalists soon shared.

Beginnings of the Anti-Federalists

While describing the Constitution as a "Social Compact" and invoking "Universal experience" to mark the value of "express declarations and reservations" of rights against "the silent, powerful, and ever active conspiracy of those who govern," Lee avoided broad statements of natural rights and first principles. Instead he detailed the specific rights that needed explicit protection: freedom of religious conscience and the press; prohibitions on excessive bail, cruel and unusual punishment, and unreasonable searches and seizures; assurances of free elections, independent judges, and the right to petition; and restrictions on standing armies in peacetime. Lee's most carefully drafted proposals, however, related to the administration of justice. Lee proposed two sets of changes to the Constitution. First, the declaration of rights he sought should affirm that the right to trial by jury in criminal and civil cases and other common-law protections in criminal prosecutions "shall be held sacred." But Lee also proposed amending Article III to assure that these general principles would be applied in detail, by providing for criminal trials "by a Jury of the Vicinage," and by preventing "the vexatious and oppressive calling of Citizens" to have their cases tried "in far distant courts," because "in a multitude of Cases, the circumstances of distance and expence may compel men to submit to the most unjust and ill founded demands." Even at this early stage of ratification, these recommendations illustrated the great sensitivity that Anti-Federalists displayed toward the administration of justice as the crucial test of the security of rights.

Federalists learned early that the omission of a bill of rights would weigh heavily against them.

Had Federalists been able to limit debate to the questions of religious conscience and the more political matters of freedom of press, assembly, elections, and standing armies, their case for the redundancy of a bill of rights would probably have proved strong enough to withstand their adversaries' claims. What would a declaration of the virtues of frequent elections or the evils of standing armies add to the constitutional provisions that already regulated these features of governance? How could matters of religious conscience ever come under federal purview—and even if they did, how could a fractious Protestant society ever agree on the norms to be enforced? But Anti-Federalist claims about the insecurity of trial by jury and other common-law rights, though more prosaic, were politically more potent. Not only did they resonate deeply in American political culture, they also exposed what was most problematic in Federalist arguments while illustrating the dilemma Americans now faced in weighing the advantages and disadvantages of grounding the authority of rights in a written constitutional text.

The Federalist Response by Wilson

While Lee was failing in his effort to convince Congress to propose amendments, the minority legislators in Pennsylvania were placing the issue of rights squarely before the public. Americans should "wonder whether the trial by jury in civil causes is become dangerous and ought to be abolished," they observed in their address of September 29 [, 1787]. James Wilson answered this charge in his public speech a week later. Smugly apologizing for having to "take advantage of my professional experience," he explained that the diversity of procedures in the states and the fact that admiralty and equity matters were resolved without juries prevented the framers from drawing a constitutional "line of discrimination" to indicate where civil juries were necessary or not. Instead they "left the business as it stands," confident that Congress, as "a faithful representation of the people," would adopt suitable regulations, and that "the oppression of government is effectually barred" by the guarantee of criminal juries.

[Patrick Henry] warned that "the Necessity of a Bill of Rights" was "greater in this Government, than ever it was in any Government before" because without it Congress would violate one right after another.

Wilson's speech proved even more controversial in its assertion that the difference between state and national constitutions obviated any need for a federal bill of rights. Accepting the social-compact imagery that dominated American thinking about the formation of the state constitutions, Wilson argued that while in the states the people had "invested their representatives with every right and authority which they did not in explicit terms reserve," in the proposed federal Constitution, "everything which is not given, is reserved." There was no need to affirm the freedom of press, for example, because nothing in the Constitution could be plausibly read to give the federal government any "power to shackle or destroy that sacred palladium of national freedom." From this position Wilson drew a further conclusion. The very insertion of a provision to protect a particular right might be falsely "construed to imply that some degree of power" to regulate its exercise "was given, since we undertook to define its extent."

Anti-Federalists Attack Wilson's Argument

In seeking to quash his opponents, Wilson miscalculated how easily they could exploit his simple if elegant distinctions between types of juries and constitutions alike. Within days Anti-Federalists were gleefully exposing the embarrassing contradiction that Wilson left open to attack. Did not the guarantee which the Constitution extended to trial by jury in criminal cases and its prohibitions against suspension of habeas corpus and the enactment of ex post facto laws comprise a partial bill of rights? If these were fundamental rights, why did they need to be mentioned in the text? And if they were explicitly recognized, were other rights not thereby rendered vulnerable to congressional regulation and even abrogation? Viewed from this perspective, the distinction between types of juries seemed to contradict the deeper distinction between state and federal constitutions on which Wilson relied. . . .

Patrick Henry's Argument for a Bill of Rights

A bill of rights was required less to guide judges in the administration of justice than to prevent Congress from voiding the common-law procedures that Americans venerated. Henry illustrated this point vividly when he warned that "the Necessity of a Bill of Rights" was "greater in this Government, than ever it was in any Government before" because without it Congress would violate one right after another. "Congress from their general powers may fully go into the business of human legislation," he claimed. "Are you not therefore now calling on those Gentlemen who are to compose Congress, to prescribe trials and define punishments without [the] controul" that Virginians enjoyed because their Declaration of Rights prohibited excessive bail and fines and cruel and unusual punishments? Without an explicit affirmation of the common law, Congress may "introduce the practice of the civil law" and the modes of torture common in France, Spain, and Germany. Its members might perhaps be trusted if they were given written "knowledge of the extent of the rights retained by the people," Henry said. "But if you leave them otherwise, they will not know how to proceed; and being in a state of uncertainty, they will assume rather than give up powers by implication."

> *Bills of rights were educational documents; they provided the standards of certainty that enabled citizens to assess doubtful acts of government.*

This was a curious conclusion to an impassioned argument, for Henry did not explain how a bill of rights would work in practice. He could not propose that it would empower the federal judges to act as vigilant guardians of rights, because the Anti-Federalist case against Article III rested on mistrust of judicial authority (though a few Anti-

Federalists, including Samuel Adams, thought a bill of rights would enable judges to check abuses of federal power). Henry instead seemed to suppose that a bill of rights would operate as a moral restraint on Congress— though if its members were as rapacious as he supposed, it was not clear why they should suddenly be reformed. Other Anti-Federalists offered a different explanation of the efficacy of a bill of rights. As John Smilie told the Pennsylvania convention, a bill of rights would provide "a plain, strong, and accurate criterion by which the people might at once determine when, and in what instance, their rights were violated" by their future "governors" and "rulers." "So loosely, so inaccurately are the powers which are enumerated in this Constitution defined, that it will be impossible, without a test of that kind, to ascertain the limits of authority and to declare when government has degenerated into oppression." The "Federal Farmer"* expressed the same idea in more abstract terms. "What is the usefulness of a truth in theory," he asked, "unless it exists constantly in the minds of the people, and has their assent?" A bill of rights did not create the rights it declared; a people were entitled to their rights "not because their ancestors once got together and enumerated them on paper, but because, by repeated negociations and declarations, all parties are brought to realize them, and of course to believe them to be sacred." The differences among societies in their attachment to rights was almost reducible to "the effect of education, a series of notions impressed upon the minds of the people by examples, precepts and declarations."

Legislative Threats

Here was a theory of rights that owed less to the *Second Treatise* than to Locke's writings on epistemology and education. Bills of rights were educational documents; they provided the standards of certainty that enabled citizens to assess doubtful acts of government; and they worked best by inculcating the values they espoused among the people *and* their rulers. But in political terms this argument still sup-

---

*The "Federal Farmer" was the author of a series of published criticisms of the proposed constitution. The articles appeared in a New York newspaper from November 1787 through January 1788. Some believe the author was Richard Henry Lee, a Virginia delegate to the Continental Congress while others think it was Melancton Smith of New York.

posed that the problem of rights was to protect the people from their governors, the ruled from their rulers. That was the traditional paradigm that few Anti-Federalists escaped. Yet the rulers whom they feared were now demonstrably those who would exercise the unbounded and indefinite legislative powers the Constitution would bestow on Congress. And in this sense at least, Anti-Federalists were no less inclined than Madison to locate the threat to rights in the power of the legislature.

There was, of course, an obvious difference between the nature of the legislative threats that Anti-Federalists and Federalists perceived. Congress was threatening in a way that the state legislatures were not, because its members lacked the accountability that enabled their provincial counterparts to fulfill their rights-protecting duty. Whether doubling or trebling the size of the House of Representatives would have left Anti-Federalists less anxious over the absence of a bill of rights is doubtful. But the structure of this debate enabled some Anti-Federalists to make the same crucial theoretical transition that drove Madison to his more radical hypotheses.

Anti-Federalists on the Need for a Written Bill of Rights

Nor was that the only leap in the theory of rights that Anti-Federalists managed to make. As faithful as they remained to tried axioms, as zealously Anglophilic as they were in naming the rights they cherished, Anti-Federalists came close to adopting a modern, positive law position on the authority that rights, however ancient or natural their origins, would have once the Constitution was ratified. By implying that traditional rights and liberties would be rendered insecure if they went undeclared, Anti-Federalists in effect suggested that the existence of these rights *depended* upon their positive expression. An American bill of rights would thus be something more than a declaration of preexisting rights; for though its adoption could be interpreted as merely verifying the birthright Americans already possessed, its omission would fatally impair their authority. Anti-Federalists sensed that the supremacy clause of a written, popularly ratified constitution could indeed sweep aside all prior claims of rights and authority. The multiple sources for the authority of rights that the colonists had once invoked now seemed obsolete because the Constitution would create its own self-sufficient standard of legality. The argument that rights would cease to be rights if they were not explicitly constitutionalized thus rested on venerable concerns, but it also addressed the modernity of the Constitution in forthright terms.

Federalists on Why a Written Bill of Rights Was Unnecessary

The Federalist response to these charges labored under two constraints, one political, the other rhetorical. The appeal for a bill of rights was not a distinct proposal in itself but part of a broader demand that the Constitution receive structural amendments prior to ratification. Federalists resisted all these appeals because they could only produce political and procedural uncertainties that would jeopardize the entire enterprise of reform. Wilson's speech created a second constraint. Even when its crucial distinctions proved vulnerable to attack, its stature as the definitive pronouncement of an authoritative commentator obliged Federalists to rally to its support. Few Federalists found this obligation troubling, however; most were probably grateful to Wilson for rebutting the Anti-Federalists in such simple but powerful terms, challenging them only to devise new metaphors to express his essential point. "To have made a formal declaration, that all the rights and powers not mentioned nor defined are reserved, would have been as great an afront to common sense," a western Massachusetts writer remarked, "as if after having made a grant of a certain tract of land . . . in a deed or bill of sale, I should add a particular enumeration of my every other piece of land and article of property, with a declaration in form, that none of these are meant to be granted." What did it matter that liberty of the press was not guaranteed? Oliver Ellsworth asked in his sixth "Landholder" essay, rebutting Mason. "Nor is liberty of conscience, or of matrimony, or of burial of the dead; it is enough that Congress have no power to prohibit either, and can have no temptation." Endless variations on this theme were possible. "As well might a Judge when he condemns a man to be hanged, give strong Injunctions to the Sheriff that he should not be beheaded."

Some of this sarcasm reflected rank annoyance with their adversaries' exploitation of this issue. Yet there is little evidence that Federalists felt embarrassed about justifying the Convention's oversight. They remained adamant that bills of rights had no place in the new federal regime; and they often extended this criticism to deny that they had any value in the states either. Their reservations echoed the criticisms that led Madison to describe bills of rights as "parchment barriers"—useless when their eloquence was arrayed against the real political forces of a republican polity and redundant when republican politics operated in its proper channels. If legislators "determined among themselves to use their efforts to effect the establishment of an aristocratical or despotick government," James Sullivan asked, "would a bill of rights be any obstacle to their proceedings?" But no less than their opponents, Federalists also confronted the fundamental question that the transition to a written constitution posed for an American theory of rights. Was the cause of liberty better served by explicitly incorporating rights in the text of a constitution, or might their enumeration and textual definition actually weaken the protection a declaration was meant to provide?

Bills of Rights in History

Federalist objections were premised on the different roles that bills of rights played in monarchies and republics. "The very words" of Magna Carta declared the rights and liberties it recognizes "to be the gift or grant of the king," Wilson reminded the Pennsylvania convention, "and under the influence of that doctrine, no wonder the people should then, and at subsequent periods, wish to obtain some concession of their formal liberties by the concessions of petitions and bills of rights." But in America "the fee simple of freedom and government is declared to be in the people." Nor did that mean that these ancient rights had been the Crown's to grant, only that the continuous challenge of recovering them from the heirs of William the Conqueror made their formal recognition all the more important. "How different then is our situation from the circumstances of the British nation?" Thomas Hartley asked the delegates at Harrisburg, for "from that instant" when independence was declared, "all our natural rights were restored to us." From this it followed "that whatever portion of those natural rights we did not transfer to the government was still reserved and retained by the people." Some rights "from their preeminence in the scale of political security, deserve to be particularly specified," Hartley concluded, but that did not negate the general point that all rights were reserved unless a positive grant of power to the government indicated otherwise. In England bills of rights were inspired by the "usurpations of the Crown," James Iredell observed, and made necessary only because "no original constitution is to be found." But had such "a solemn instrument delegat[ing] particular powers to the Crown at the formation of their government" existed in England, no bill of rights would have been required even there. The Declaration of 1689 was a poor model for Americans to imitate; its articles "were never intended to limit the authority of Parliament." Bills of rights had been "eagerly adopted" by the states "without a due attention to the difference of the cases," at a moment when "the minds of men then being so warmed with their exertions in the cause of liberty, as to lean too much towards a jealousy of power to repose a proper confidence in their own government."

There is little evidence that Federalists felt embarrassed about justifying the Convention's oversight.

Nothing would have been lost, then, had the states omitted to declare rights in 1776; liberty was as secure in those states which lacked bills of rights, Wilson told the Pennsylvania ratifiers, as in those that had adopted them. The true security lay in the system of representation, the mutuality of interests between legislators and electors, and the virtue of a people whose liberties "never can be lost," a Virginia writer declared, "until they are lost to themselves, in a vicious disregard of their dearest interests, a sottish indolence, a wild licentiousness, a dissoluteness of morals, and a contempt of all virtue." "No bill of rights ever yet bound the supreme power longer than the *honey moon* of a new married couple, unless the *rulers were interested* in preserving the rights," Roger Sherman wrote in his second "Countryman" letter. "The sole question . . . ought to be, how are Congress formed? how far are the members interested to preserve your rights? How far have you a controul over them?" Hamilton nearly reduced this argument to a single sentence when he asserted that "the Constitution is itself, in every rational sense, and to every useful purpose, A BILL OF RIGHTS." Like most Federalists, he found the clamor for a bill of rights hard to credit; his treatment of the topic in *Federalist* 84 was essentially an afterthought that restated conventional arguments. . . .

Hamilton and the Federalist Concern About Listing Rights

Alexander Hamilton nonetheless followed other Federalists in insisting that a more thorough rendering of rights would prove "not only unnecessary in the proposed Constitution, but would even be dangerous." The two realms where this danger was most likely to arise, Federalists generally insisted, were liberty of the press and freedom of conscience. How could one affirm that either right was to be protected, Hamilton asked, without conveying "a clear implication, that a power to prescribe proper regulations concerning it was intended to be vested in the national government"?

The force of this objection reflected the deeper tendency in eighteenth-century thinking to regard rights not as absolute barriers against public regulation but rather as guarantees that when the state acted it must do so lawfully. But the Federalist concern was directed to a more profound issue. If one began with the premise that rights were properly secure only when explicitly protected, it followed that any enumeration undertaken to rectify the omissions of the Convention would have to be comprehensive or risk creating new dangers of its own. Had the framers assumed the laborious task of enumerating "every thing, which the citizens of the United States claim as a natural or civic right," Alexander Contee Hanson wrote, they would have exposed the Constitution to greater criticism, for "[a]n omission of a single article would have caused more discontent, than is either felt, or pretended, on the present occasion." Moreover, such an effort might suffer not only from partiality but also from an unavoidable lack of foresight. If a bill of rights was indeed necessary to erect the standard to which the people must resort to judge their rulers, it had to be drawn with the greatest care, Jasper Yeates told the Pennsylvania ratifiers, "for, it might be argued at a future day by the persons then in power—you undertook to enumerate the rights which you mean to reserve, the pretension which you make is not comprised in that enumeration, and, consequently, our jurisdiction is not circumscribed." Nor was omission the only danger. "Our rights are not yet all known," Benjamin Rush told the Pennsylvania convention; how then could they be properly enumerated?

Hamilton nearly reduced this argument to a single sentence when he asserted that "the Constitution is itself, in every rational sense, and to every useful purpose, A BILL OF RIGHTS."

To prove the absurdity of enumerating rights, Federalists lampooned one of the amendments proposed by the minority in the Pennsylvania convention, which would have affirmed that Americans would retain the "liberty to fowl and hunt in seasonable times, and on lands they hold ... and in like manner to fish in all navigable waters, and others not private property, without being restrained" by Congress. Nearly transported by "laughter at this clause," Noah Webster proposed a further "restriction:—'That Congress shall never restrain any inhabitant of America from eating and drinking, *at seasonable times,* or prevent his lying on his *left side,* in a long winter's night, or even on his back, when he is fatigued by lying on his *right.'*" Such barbs came easily to Federalist jesters, but the issue both sides addressed remained serious enough. By specifying some rights, the framers had obviously not meant to disparage others, least of all venerable common-law procedures. But a lack of sinister intentions just as obviously did not obviate the theoretical problem of determining whether the Constitution had left the glass of rights half empty, half full—or full. As exaggerated as Anti-Federalist fears were, they confronted a theoretical problem of the first magnitude. Once a partial set of rights had received textual recognition as supreme law, did that not relegate all other rights to some lesser or more problematic status, even if they were originally derived from the variety of preexisting sources to which the colonists had appealed before 1776?

4

The Constitution Does Not Need a Bill of Rights

Alexander Hamilton

During the American Revolution, Alexander Hamilton fought in two campaigns and became George Washington's secretary. After the war, he represented New York in Congress and was a vigorous spokesman for a strong national government at the Constitutional Convention in 1787. Alarmed by the virulent criticism of the proposed Constitution by New York papers, Hamilton decided to write a series of essays in defense of the document. He succeeded in adding two other writers to help him—John Jay and James Madison. The *Federalist* papers that resulted exerted tremendous influence and became classics of eighteenth-century political writing. In the following excerpt from *The Federalist #84*, Hamilton responds to the claim by anti-Federalists that the Constitution needs a bill of rights. He argues that the proposed Constitution adequately protects Americans without a bill of rights. He then explains that bills of rights originated in monarchal governments in which a king had all the power and the people had only those rights that were expressly given. In contrast, he says, under the American Constitution the people have the power and surrender no rights in the formation of the new government. In addition, Hamilton claims a bill of rights would actually be dangerous because it might falsely indicate that the Constitution had given more power to the national government than it actually had. He ends the excerpt by claiming the entire Constitution is a bill of rights itself in its description of the structure and function of government.

Excerpted from *The Federalist #84*, by Alexander Hamilton, May 28, 1788.

In the course of the foregoing review of the constitution I have taken notice of, and endeavoured to answer, most of the objections which have appeared against it. There however remain a few which either did not fall naturally under any particular head, or were forgotten in their proper places. These shall now be discussed; but as the subject has been drawn into great length, I shall so far consult brevity as to comprise all my observations on these miscellaneous points in a single paper.

The most considerable of these remaining objections is, that the plan of the convention contains no bill of rights. Among other answers given to this, it has been upon different occasions remarked, that the constitutions of several of the states are in a similar predicament. I add, that New-York is of this number. And yet the opposers of the new system in this state, who profess an unlimited admiration for its constitution, are among the most intemperate partizans of a bill of rights. To justify their zeal in this matter, they alledge two things; one is, that though the constitution of New-York has no bill of rights prefixed to it, yet it contains in the body of it various provisions in favour of particular privileges and rights, which in substance amount to the same thing; the other is, that the constitution adopts in their full extent the common and statute law of Great-Britain, by which many other rights not expressed in it are equally secured.

The Constitution Contains Rights

To the first I answer that the constitution proposed by the convention contains, as well as the constitution of this state, a number of such provisions.

Independent of those, which relate to the structure of the government, we find the following: Article I. section 3. clause 7. "Judgment in cases of impeachment shall not extend further than to removal from office, and disqualification to hold and enjoy any office of honour, trust or profit under the United States; but the party convicted shall nevertheless be liable and subject to indictment, trial, judgment and punishment, according to law." Section 9. of the same article, clause 2. "The privilege of the writ of *habeas corpus* shall not be suspended, unless when in cases of rebellion or invasion the public safety may require it." Clause 3. "No bill of attainder or *ex post facto* law shall be passed." Clause 7. "No title of nobility shall be granted by the United States: And no person holding any office of profit or trust under them, shall, without the consent of the congress, accept of any present, emolument, office or title, of any kind whatever, from any king, prince or foreign state." Article III. section 2. clause 3. "The trial of all crimes, except in cases of impeachment, shall be by jury; and such trial shall be held in the state where the said crimes shall have been committed; but when not committed within any state, the trial shall be at such place or places as the congress may by law have directed." Section 3, of the same article, "Treason against the United States shall consist only in levying war against them, or in adhering to their enemies, giving them aid and comfort. No person shall be convicted of treason unless on the testimony of two witnesses to the same overt act, or on confession in open court."

Alexander Hamilton

And clause 3, of the same section. "The congress shall have power to declare the punishment of treason, but no attainder of treason shall work corruption of blood, or forfeiture, except during the life of the person attainted.". . .

Difference Between British and American Rights

To the pretended establishment of the common and statute law by the constitution, I answer, that they are expressly made subject "to such alterations and provisions as the legislature shall from time to time make concerning the same." They are therefore at any moment liable to repeal by the ordinary legislative power, and of course have no constitutional sanction. The only use of the declaration was to recognize the ancient law, and to remove doubts which might have been occasioned by the revolution. This consequently can be considered as no part of a declaration of rights, which under our constitutions must be intended as limitations of the power of government itself.

It has been several times truly remarked, that bills of

rights are in their origin, stipulations between kings and their subjects, abridgments of prerogative in favor of privilege, reservations of rights not surrendered to the prince. Such was MAGNA CHARTA, obtained by the Barons, sword in hand, from king John. Such were the subsequent confirmations of that charter by subsequent princes. Such was the *petition of right* assented to by Charles the First, in the beginning of his reign. Such also was the declaration of right presented by the lords and commons to the prince of Orange in 1688, and afterwards thrown into the form of an act of parliament, called the bill of rights. It is evident, therefore, that according to their primitive signification, they have no application to constitutions professedly founded upon the power of the people, and executed by their immediate representatives and servants. Here, in strictness, the people surrender nothing, and as they retain every thing, they have no need of particular reservations. "WE THE PEOPLE of the United States, to secure the blessings of liberty to ourselves and our posterity, do *ordain* and *establish* this constitution for the United States of America." Here is a better recognition of popular rights than volumes of those aphorisms which make the principal figure in several of our state bills of rights, and which would sound much better in a treatise of ethics than in a constitution of government.

But a minute detail of particular rights is certainly far less applicable to a constitution like that under consideration, which is merely intended to regulate the general political interests of the nation, than to a constitution which has the regulation of every species of personal and private concerns. If therefore the loud clamours against the plan of the convention on this score, are well founded, no epithets of reprobation will be too strong for the constitution of this state. But the truth is, that both of them contain all, which in relation to their objects, is reasonably to be desired.

Danger of a Bill of Rights

I go further, and affirm that bills of rights, in the sense and in the extent in which they are contended for, are not only unnecessary in the proposed constitution, but would even be dangerous. They would contain various exceptions to powers which are not granted; and on this very account, would afford a colourable pretext to claim more than were granted. For why declare that things shall not be done which there is no power to do? Why for instance, should it be said, that the liberty of the press shall not be restrained, when no power is given by which restrictions may be imposed? I will not contend that such a provision would confer a regulating power; but it is evident that it would furnish, to men disposed to usurp, a plausible pretence for claiming that power. They might urge with a semblance of reason, that the constitution ought not to be charged with the absurdity of providing against the abuse of an authority, which was not given, and that the provision against restraining the liberty of the press afforded a clear implication, that a power to prescribe proper regulations concerning it, was intended to be vested in the national government. This may serve as a specimen of the numerous handles which would be given to the doctrine of constructive powers, by the indulgence of an injudicious zeal for bills of rights.

Liberty of the Press

On the subject of the liberty of the press, as much has been said, I cannot forbear adding a remark or two: In the first place, I observe that there is not a syllable concerning it in the constitution of this state, and in the next, I contend that whatever has been said about it in that of any other state, amounts to nothing. What signifies a declaration that "the liberty of the press shall be inviolably preserved?" What is the liberty of the press? Who can give it any definition which would not leave the utmost latitude for evasion? I hold it to be impracticable; and from this, I infer, that its security, whatever fine declarations may be inserted in any constitution respecting it, must altogether depend on public opinion, and on the general spirit of the people and of the government. And here, after all, as intimated upon another occasion, must we seek for the only solid basis of all our rights.

Constitution Is a Bill of Rights

There remains but one other view of this matter to conclude the point. The truth is, after all the declamation we have heard, that the constitution is itself in every rational sense, and to every useful purpose, A BILL OF RIGHTS. The several bills of rights, in Great-Britain, form its constitution, and conversely the constitution of each state is its bill of rights. And the proposed constitution, if adopted, will be the bill of rights of the union. Is it one object of a bill of rights to declare and specify the political privileges of the citizens in the structure and administration of the government? This is done in the most ample and precise manner in the plan of the convention, comprehending various precautions for the public security, which are not to be found in any of the state constitutions. Is another object of a bill of rights to define certain immunities and modes of proceeding, which are relative to personal and private concerns? This we have seen has also been attended to, in a variety of cases, in the same plan. Advertising therefore to the substantial meaning of a bill of rights, it is absurd to allege that it is not to be found in the work of the convention. It may be said that it does not go far enough, though it will not be easy to make this appear; but it can with no propriety be contended that there is no such thing. It certainly must be immaterial what mode is observed as to the order of declaring the rights of the citizens, if they are to be found in any part of the instrument which establishes the government. And hence it must be apparent that much of what has been said on this subject rests merely on verbal and nominal distinctions, which are entirely foreign from the substance of the thing.

5

The Constitution Needs a Bill of Rights

"Brutus"

"Brutus," the pseudonym of a man presumed to be Robert Yates of New York, published his essays against the proposed Constitution in a New York paper between October 1787 and April 1788. His essays probably influenced Alexander Hamilton to defend the Constitution in the *Federalist* papers. In the following selection, "Brutus" explains that the country needs a bill of rights because of the history of governmental abuses. Over the long span of human history, he writes, governments have tended to expand their powers at the expense of the people. Unlike Alexander Hamilton, he argues that the federal government has been given a great deal of power under the proposed Constitution. He outlines key rights that the states have enumerated and insists the federal government should also explicitly protect these rights.

Those who have governed, have been found in all ages ever active to enlarge their powers and abridge the public liberty. This has induced the people in all countries, where any sense of freedom remained, to fix barriers against the encroachments of their rulers. The country from which we have derived our origin, is an eminent example of this. Their magna charta and bill of rights have long been the boast, as well as the security, of that nation. I need say no more, I presume, to an American, then, that this principle is a fundamental one, in all the constitutions of our own states; there is not one of them but what is either founded on a

Excerpted from "Brutus No. 2," *New York Journal*, November 1, 1787.

declaration or bill of rights, or has certain express reservation of rights interwoven in the body of them. From this it appears, that at a time when the pulse of liberty beat high and when an appeal was made to the people to form constitutions for the government of themselves, it was their universal sense, that such declarations should make a part of their frames of government. It is therefore the more astonishing, that this grand security, to the rights of the people, is not to be found in this constitution.

It has been said, in answer to this objection, that such declaration(s) of rights, however requisite they might be in the constitutions of the states, are not necessary in the general constitution, because, "in the former case, everything which is not reserved is given, but in the latter the reverse of the proposition prevails, and every thing which is not given is reserved." It requires but little attention to discover, that this mode of reasoning is rather specious than solid. The powers, rights, and authority, granted to the general government by this constitution, are as complete, with respect to every object to which they extend, as that of any state government—It reaches to every thing which concerns human happiness—Life, liberty, and property, are under its controul. There is the same reason, therefore, that the exercise of power, in this case, should be restrained within proper limits, as in that of the state governments. To set this matter in a clear light, permit me to instance some of the articles of the bills of rights of the individual states, and apply them to the case in question.

Trial Rights

For the security of life, in criminal prosecutions, the bills of rights of most of the states have declared, that no man shall be held to answer for a crime until he is made fully acquainted with the charge brought against him; he shall not be compelled to accuse, or furnish evidence against himself—The witnesses against him shall be brought face to face, and he shall be fully heard by himself or counsel. That it is essential to the security of life and liberty, that trial of facts be in the vicinity where they happen. Are not provisions of this kind as necessary in the general government, as in that of a particular state? The powers vested in the new Congress extend in many cases to life; they are authorised to provide for the punishment of a variety of capital crimes, and no restraint is laid upon them in its exercise, save only, that "the trial of all crimes, except in cases of impeachment, shall be by jury; and such trial shall be in the state where the said crimes shall have been committed." No man is secure of a trial in the county where he is charged to have committed a crime; he may be brought from Niagara to New-York, or carried from Kentucky to Richmond for trial for an offence, supposed to be committed. What security is there, that a man shall be furnished with a full and plain description of the charges against him? That he shall be allowed to produce all proof he can in his favor? That he shall see the witnesses against him face to face, or that he shall be fully heard in his own defence by himself or counsel?

It is . . . astonishing, that this grand security, to the rights of the people, is not to be found in this constitution.

For the security of liberty it has been declared, "that excessive bail should not be required, nor excessive fines imposed, nor cruel or unusual punishments inflicted—That all warrants, without oath or affirmation, to search suspected places, or seize any person, his papers or property, are grievous and oppressive."

These provisions are as necessary under the general government as under that of the individual states; for the power of the former is as complete to the purpose of requiring bail, imposing fines, inflicting punishments, granting search warrants, and seizing persons, papers, or property, in certain cases, as the other.

For the purpose of securing the property of the citizens, it is declared by all the states, "that in all controversies at law, respecting property, the ancient mode of trial by jury is one of the best securities of the rights of the people, and ought to remain sacred and inviolable."

Controul of the Armies

Does not the same necessity exist of reserving this right, under this national compact, as in that of these states? Yet nothing is said respecting it. In the bills of rights of the states it is declared, that a well regulated militia is the proper and natural defence of a free government—That as standing armies in time of peace are dangerous, they are not to be kept up, and that the military should be kept under strict subordination to, and controuled by the civil power.

The same security is as necessary in this constitution, and much more so; for the general government will have the sole power to raise and to pay armies, and are under no controul in the exercise of it; yet nothing of this is to be found in this new system.

Exceptions

I might proceed to instance a number of other rights, which were as necessary to be reserved, such as, that elections should be free, that the liberty of the press should be held sacred; but the instances adduced, are sufficient to prove, that this argument is without foundation.—Besides, it is evident, that the reason here assigned was not the true one, why the framers of this constitution omitted a bill of rights; if it had been, they would not have made certain reservations, while they totally omitted others of more importance. We find they have, in the 9th section of the 1st article, declared, that the writ of habeas corpus shall not be suspended, unless in cases of rebellion—that no bill of attainder, or expost facto law, shall be passed—that no title of nobility shall be granted by the United States, &c. If every thing which is not given is reserved, what propriety is there in these exceptions? Does this constitution any where grant the power of suspending the habeas corpus, to make expost facto laws, pass bills of attainder, or grant titles of nobility? It certainly does not in express terms. The only answer that can be given is, that these are implied in the general powers granted. With equal truth it may be said, that all the powers, which the bills of right, guard against the abuse of, are contained or implied in the general ones granted by this constitution.

It was of the highest importance, that the most precise and express declarations and reservations of rights should have been made.

So far it is from being true, that a bill of rights is less necessary in the general constitution than in those of the states, the contrary is evidently the fact.—This system, if it is possible for the people of America to accede to it, will be an original compact; and being the last, will, in the nature of things, vacate every former agreement inconsistent with it. For it being a plan of government received and ratified by the whole people, all other forms, which are in existence at the time of its adoption, must yield to it. This is expressed in positive and unequivocal terms, in the 6th article, "That this constitution and the laws of the United States, which shall be made in pursuance thereof, and all treaties made, or which shall be made, under the authority of the United States, shall be the supreme law of the land; and the judges in every state shall be bound thereby, any thing in the *constitution*, or laws of any state, *to the contrary* notwithstanding.

"The senators and representatives before-mentioned, and the members of the several state legislatures, and all executive and judicial officers, both of the United States, and of the several states, shall be bound, by oath or affirmation, to support this constitution."

Supremacy of the Constitution

It is therefore not only necessarily implied thereby, but positively expressed, that the different state constitutions are repealed and entirely done away, so far as they are inconsistent with this, with the laws which shall be made in pursuance thereof, or with treaties made, or which shall be made, under the authority of the United States; of what avail will the constitutions of the respective states be to preserve the rights of its citizens? should they be plead, the answer would be, the constitution of the United States, and the laws made in pursuance thereof, is the supreme law, and all legislatures and judicial officers, whether of the general or state governments, are bound by oath to support it. No priviledge, reserved by the bills of rights, or secured by the state government, can limit the power granted by this, or restrain any laws made in pursuance of it. It stands therefore on its own bottom, and must receive a construction by itself without any reference to any other—And hence it was of the highest importance, that the most precise and express declarations and reservations of rights should have been made.

This will appear the more necessary, when it is considered, that not only the constitution and laws made in pursuance thereof, but all treaties made, or which shall be made, under the authority of the United States, are the supreme law of the land, and supersede the constitutions of all the states. The power to make treaties, is vested in the president, by and with the advice and consent of two thirds of the senate. I do not find any limitation, or restriction, to the exercise of this power. The most important article in any constitution may therefore be repealed, even without a legislative act. Ought not a government, vested with such extensive and indefinite authority, to have been restricted by a declaration of rights? It certainly ought.

So clear a point is this, that I cannot help suspecting, that persons who attempt to persuade people, that such reservations were less necessary under this constitution than under those of the states, are wilfully endeavouring to deceive, and to lead you into an absolute state of vassalage.

6

Without a Bill of Rights, the Government Is Too Powerful

Patrick Henry

Patrick Henry was a distinguished statesman and orator who is remembered for the firm stance he took in support of revolution when he said, "Give me liberty or give me death." During the Revolutionary War he served as governor of Virginia. Later he was part of the Virginia state convention called to ratify the United States Constitution. The selection that follows is taken from remarks he made during this convention. He opposed the new form of government, believing that a lack of a bill of rights endangered the citizens by granting too much power to the national government. He focuses on the value of a bill of rights to protect citizens' rights to receive a fair trial and to be free of unfair searches and seizures.

16 June 1788

Mr. Chairman.—The necessity of a Bill of Rights appear to me to be greater in this Government, than ever it was in any Government before. . . .

All nations have adopted this construction—That all rights not expressly and unequivocally reserved to the people, are impliedly and incidentally relinquished to rulers; as necessarily inseparable from the delegated powers. It is so in Great-Britain: For every possible right which is not reserved to the people by some express provision or compact, is within the King's prerogative. It is so in that country

Excerpted from *Debates and Other Proceedings of the Convention of Virginia*, edited by David Robertson (Petersburg, VA: 1788).

which is said to be in such full possession of freedom. It is so in Spain, Germany, and other parts of the world.

America, Its Revolution, and Its Rights

Let us consider the sentiments which have been entertained by the people of America on this subject. At the revolution, it must be admitted, that it was their sense to put down those great rights which ought in all countries to be held inviolable and sacred. Virginia did so we all remember. She made a compact to reserve, expressly, certain rights. When fortified with full, adequate, and abundant representation, was she satisfied with that representation? No.—She most cautiously and guardedly reserved and secured those invaluable, inestimable rights and privileges, which no people, inspired with the least glow of the patriotic love of liberty, ever did, or ever can, abandon. She is called upon now to abandon them, and dissolve that compact which secured them to her. She is called upon to accede to another compact which most infallibly supercedes and annihilates her present one. Will she do it?—This is the question. If you intend to reserve your unalienable rights, you must have the most express stipulation. For if implication be allowed, you are ousted of those rights. If the people do not think it necessary to reserve them, they will be supposed to be given up. How were the Congressional rights defined when the people of America united by a confederacy to defend their liberties and rights against the tyrannical attempts of Great-Britain? The States were not then contented with implied reservation. No, Mr. Chairman. It was expressly declared in our Confederation that every right was retained by the States respectively, which was not given up to the Government of the United States. But there is no such thing here. You therefore by a natural and unavoidable implication, give up your rights to the General Government. Your own example furnishes an argument against it. If you give up these powers, without a Bill of Rights, you will exhibit the most absurd thing to mankind that ever the world saw—A Government that has abandoned all its powers—The powers of direct taxation, the sword, and the purse. You have disposed of them to Congress, without a Bill of Rights—without check, limitation, or controul. And still you have checks and guards—still you keep barriers—pointed where? Pointed against your weakened, prostrated, enervated State Government! You have a Bill of Rights to defend you against the State Government, which is bereaved of all power; and yet you have none against Congress, though in full and exclusive possession of all power! You arm yourselves against the weak and defenceless, and expose yourselves naked to the armed and powerful. Is not this a conduct of unexampled absurdity? What barriers have you to oppose to this most strong energetic Government? To that Government you have nothing to oppose. All your defence is given up. This is a real actual defect.—It must strike the mind of every Gentleman. When our Government was first instituted in Virginia, we declared the common law of England to be in force.—That system of law which has been admired, and has protected us and our ancestors, is excluded by that system.—Added to this, we adopted a Bill of Rights. By this Constitution, some of the best barriers of human rights are thrown away. Is there not an additional reason to have a Bill of Rights? By the ancient common law, the trial of all facts is decided by a jury of impartial men from the immediate vicinage. This paper speaks of different juries from the common law, in criminal cases; and in civil controversies excludes trial by jury altogether. There is therefore more occasion for the supplementary check of a Bill of Rights now, than then. Congress from their general powers may fully go

Patrick Henry, pictured here during a 1775 speech, believed that a bill of rights was necessary for the protection of citizens' rights.

into the business of human legislation. They may legislate
in criminal cases from treason to the lowest offence, petty
larceny. They may define crimes and prescribe punishments. In the definition of crimes, I trust they will be directed by what wise Representatives ought to be governed
by. But when we come to punishments, no latitude ought to
be left, nor dependence put on the virtue of Representatives. What says our Bill of Rights? "That excessive bail
ought not to be required, nor excessive fines imposed, nor
cruel and unusual punishments inflicted." Are you not
therefore now calling on those Gentlemen who are to compose Congress, to prescribe trials and define punishments
without this controul? Will they find sentiments there similar to this Bill of Rights? You let them loose—you do
more—you depart from the genius of your country. That
paper tells you, that the trial of crimes shall be by jury, and
held in the State where the crime shall have been committed.—Under this extensive provision, they may proceed in a
manner extremely dangerous to liberty.—Persons accused
may be carried from one extremity of the State to another,
and be tried not by an impartial jury of the vicinage, acquainted with his character, and the circumstances of the
fact; but by a jury unacquainted with both, and who may be
biassed against him.—Is not this sufficient to alarm men?—
How different is this from the immemorial practice of your
British ancestors, and your own? I need not tell you, that by
the [English] common law a number of hundredors [resi-
dents from the same group of one hundred] were required
to be on a jury, and that afterwards it was sufficient if the jurors came from the same county. With less than this the
people of England have never been satisfied. That paper
ought to have declared the common law in force. . . .

Value of a Bill of Rights

A Bill of Rights may be summed up in a few words. What
do they tell us?—That our rights are reserved.—Why not
say so? Is it because it will consume too much paper? Gentlemen's reasonings against a Bill of Rights, do not satisfy
me. Without saying which has the right side, it remains
doubtful. A Bill of Rights is a favourite thing with the Virginians, and the people of the other States likewise. It may
be their prejudice but the Government ought to suit their
geniuses, otherwise its operation will be unhappy. A Bill of

Rights, even if its necessity be doubtful, will exclude the possibility of dispute, and with great submission, I think the best way is to have no dispute. In the present Constitution, they are restrained from issuing general warrants to search suspected places, or seize persons not named, without evidence of the commission of the fact, &c. There was certainly some celestial influence governing those who deliberated on that Constitution:—For they have with the most cautious and enlightened circumspection, guarded those indefeasible rights, which ought ever to be held sacred. The officers of Congress may come upon you, fortified with all the terrors of paramount federal authority.—Excisemen may come in multitudes:—For the limitation of their numbers no man knows.—They may, unless the General Government be restrained by a Bill of Rights, or some similar restriction, go into your cellars and rooms, and search, ransack and measure, every thing you eat, drink and wear. They ought to be restrained within proper bounds. With respect to the freedom of the press, I need say nothing; for it is hoped that the Gentlemen who shall compose Congress, will take care as little as possible, to infringe the rights of human nature.—This will result from their integrity. They should from prudence, abstain from violating the rights of their constituents. They are not however expressly restrained.—But whether they will intermeddle with that palladium of our liberties or not, I leave you to determine. . . .

My mind will not be quieted till I see something substantial come forth in the shape of a Bill of Rights.

7

The People's Rights Are Protected Without a Bill of Rights

Edmund Randolph

Edmund Randolph served as George Washington's aide-de-camp during the Revolutionary War. After serving in the Continental Congress, he was elected governor of Virginia in 1786. At the Constitutional Convention he proposed the Virginia Plan, which favored the large states. When the members rejected this plan, he refused to sign the Constitution. Like Patrick Henry, he served as a member of the Virginia state convention called to ratify the Constitution. But unlike Henry, he urged the state to accept the new form of government. In the following selection he argues against Henry by saying there is no need for a bill of rights because essential rights are protected by the Constitution.

───────────────────────────

At the beginning of the war we had no certain Bill of Rights: For our charter cannot be considered as a Bill of Rights. It is nothing more than an investiture in the hands of the Virginian citizens, of those rights which belonged to the British subjects. When the British thought proper to infringe our rights, was it not necessary to mention in our Constitution, those rights which ought to be paramount to the power of the legislature? Why are the Bill of Rights distinct from the Constitution? I consider Bills of Rights in this view, that the Government should use them when there is a departure from its fundamental principles,

Excerpted from *The Debate on the Constitution: Federalist and Antifederalist Speeches, Articles, and Letters During the Struggle over Ratification*, vol. 2 (New York: The Library of America, 1993).

58

in order to restore them. This is the true sense of a Bill of Rights. If it be consistent with the Constitution, or contains additional rights, why not put it in the Constitution? If it be repugnant to the Constitution, there will be a perpetual scene of warfare between them. The Honorable Gentleman has praised the Bill of Rights of Virginia, and called it his guardian angel, and vilified this Constitution for not having it. Give me leave to make a distinction between the Representatives of the people of a particular country, who are appointed as the ordinary Legislature, having no limitation to their powers, and another body arising from a compact and certain delineated powers. Were a Bill of Rights necessary in the former, it would not in the latter; for the best security that can be in the latter is the express enumeration of its powers. But let me ask the Gentleman where his favourite rights are violated? They are not violated by the tenth section, which contains restrictions on the States. Are they violated by the enumerated powers? (Here his Excellency read from the eighth to the twelfth article of the Declaration of Rights.)—Is there not provision made in this Constitution for the trial by jury in criminal cases? Does not the third article provide, that the trial of all crimes shall be by jury, and held in the State where the said crimes shall have been committed? Does it not follow, that the cause and nature of the accusation must be produced, because otherwise they cannot proceed on the cause? Every one knows, that the witnesses must be brought before the jury, or else the prisoner will be discharged. Calling for evidence in his favor is co-incident to his trial. There is no suspicion, that less than twelve jurors will be thought sufficient. The only defect is, that there is no speedy trial.—Consider how this could have been amended. We have heard complaints against it, because it is supposed the jury is to come from the State at large. It will be in their power to have juries from the vicinage. And would not the complaints have been louder, if they had appointed a Federal Court to be had in every county in the State?—Criminals are brought in this State from every part of the country to the General Court, and jurors from the vicinage are summoned to the trials. There can be no reason to prevent the General Government from adopting a similar regulation.

As to the exclusion of excessive bail and fines, and cruel and unusual punishments, this would follow of itself without a Bill of Rights. Observations have been made about watchfulness over those in power, which deserve our attention. There must be a combination—We must presume corruption in the House of Representatives, Senate, and President, before we can suppose that excessive fines can be imposed, or cruel punishments inflicted. Their number is the highest security.—Numbers are the highest security in our own Constitution, which has attracted so many eulogiums from the Gentleman. Here we have launched into a sea of suspicions. How shall we check power?—By their numbers. Before these cruel punishments can be inflicted, laws must be passed, and Judges must judge contrary to justice. This would excite universal discontent, and detestation of the Members of the Government. They might involve their friends in the calamities resulting from it, and could be removed from office. I never desire a greater security than this, which I believe to be absolutely sufficient.

Remember we were not making a Constitution for Virginia alone. . . . But we were forming a Constitution for thirteen States.

That general warrants are grievous and oppressive, and ought not to be granted, I fully admit. I heartily concur in expressing my detestation of them. But we have sufficient security here also. We do not rely on the integrity of any one particular person or body; but on the number and different orders of the Members of the Government: Some of them having necessarily the same feelings with ourselves. Can it be believed, that the Federal Judiciary would not be independent enough to prevent such oppressive practices? If they will not do justice to persons injured, may they not go to our own State Judiciaries and obtain it?

Gentlemen have been misled to a certain degree, by a general declaration, that the trial by jury was gone. We see that in the most valuable cases, it is reserved. Is it abolished in civil cases? Let him put his finger on the part where it is abolished. The Constitution is silent on it.—What expression would you wish the Constitution to use, to establish it? Remember we were not making a Constitution for Virginia alone, or we might have taken Virginia for our directory. But we were forming a Constitution for thirteen States. The trial by jury is different in different States. In some States it is excluded in cases in which it is admitted in others. In Admiralty causes it is not used. Would you have a jury to determine the case of a capture? The Virginian Legislature thought proper to make an exception of that case. These depend on the law of nations, and no twelve men that could be picked up would be equal to the decision of such a matter.

Freedom of the Press and Religion

Then, Sir, the freedom of the press is said to be insecure. God forbid that I should give my voice against the freedom of the press. But I ask, (and with confidence that it cannot be answered) where is the page where it is restrained? If there had been any regulation about it, leaving it insecure, then there might have been reason for clamours. But this is not the case. If it be, I again ask for the particular clause which gives liberty to destroy the freedom of the press.

He has added religion to the objects endangered in his conception. Is there any power given over it? Let it be pointed out. Will he not be contented with the answer which has been frequently given to that objection? That variety of sects which abounds in the United States is the best security for the freedom of religion. No part of the Constitution, even if strictly construed, will justify a conclusion, that the General Government can take away, or impair the freedom of religion.

Though I do not reverence the Constitution, . . . its adoption is necessary to avoid the storm which is hanging over America.

The Gentleman asks with triumph, shall we be deprived of these valuable rights? Had there been an exception, or express infringement of those rights, he might object.—But I conceive every fair reasoner will agree, that there is no just cause to suspect that they will be violated. . . .

Need to Adopt the Constitution to Save the Country

I cast my eyes to the actual situation of America; I see the dreadful tempest, to which the present calm is a prelude, if disunion takes place. I see the anarchy which must happen if no energetic Government be established. In this situation, I would take the Constitution were it more objectionable than it is.—For if anarchy and confusion follow disunion, an enterprising man may enter into the American throne. I conceive there is no danger. The Representatives are chosen by and from among the people. They will have a fellow-feeling for the farmers and planters. The twenty-six Senators, Representatives of the States, will not be those desperadoes and horrid adventurers which they are represented to be. The State Legislatures, I trust, will not forget the duty they owe to their country so far, as to choose such men to manage their federal interests. I trust, that the Members of Congress themselves, will explain the ambiguous parts: And if not, the States can combine in order to insist on amending the ambiguities. I would depend on the present actual feelings of the people of America, to introduce any amendment which may be necessary. I repeat it again, though I do not reverence the Constitution, that its adoption is necessary to avoid the storm which is hanging over America, and that no greater curse can befal her, than the dissolution of the political connection between the States. Whether we shall propose previous or subsequent amendments, is now the only dispute. It is supererogation to repeat again the arguments in support of each.—But I ask Gentlemen, whether, as eight States have adopted it, it be not safer to adopt it, and rely on the probability of obtaining amendments, than by a rejection to hazard a breach of the Union? I hope to be excused for the breach of order which I have committed.

8

The Bill of Rights
Becomes Law

Richard B. Bernstein and Jerome Agel

Richard B. Bernstein, a professor of law at New York Law
School, has written or edited twelve books on American constitutional history. Jerome Agel has written or produced more
than fifty books. In the selection that follows, they describe
James Madison's activities in the first session of Congress
(1788). Madison at one time opposed a bill of rights, but now
he favored such an addition to the Constitution. The authors
explore his reasons for opposing a bill of rights and for later
changing his mind. They then lead the reader through the difficult process by which Madison was able to get the Congress
to pass the amendments and the struggle that took place when
the states debated their inclusion in the Constitution.

L eadership to obtain a bill of rights from the First Congress came from someone who, only a year earlier,
would have been a most unlikely candidate for the role.
James Madison had reversed his stand from the opening
stages of the struggle for ratification, having made a public
commitment at the Virginia ratifying convention to work to
amend the Constitution. This about-face was the most
noteworthy development in the ratification controversy
with respect to future amendments. Madison brought many
strengths to the movement for a declaration of rights: his
national political stature, his ability to secure President
Washington's backing of the call for amendments securing

Excerpted from *Amending America*, by Richard B. Bernstein and Jerome Agel
(New York: Times Books, 1993). Copyright © 1993 by Richard B. Bernstein and
Jerome Agel. Reprinted with permission.

individual rights, and his extraordinary intellectual talents and capacity for hard work.

Madison's Opposition to the Bill of Rights

At first Madison had been cool to the idea of adding a bill of rights to the Constitution. His experience of Virginia politics in the 1780s, and his scrutiny of politics on both state and national levels, had led him to conclude that a bill of rights would be a mere "parchment barrier," insufficient to restrain a government or a popular majority bent on violating rights. Madison explained his thinking in a letter to Thomas Jefferson in 1788:

> [E]xperience proves the inefficacy of a bill of rights on those occasions when its controul is most needed. Repeated violations of these *parchment barriers* have been committed by overbearing majorities in every State.

Such arguments carried great force, especially among veterans of the tumultuous state politics of the 1780s, who had seen firsthand the ineffectiveness of state constitutional provisions guaranteeing rights against determined legislative and popular majorities. . . .

Madison brought many strengths to the movement for a declaration of rights.

It is not surprising that Madison found the "parchment barriers" argument congenial. He believed that the plan for representation in the national legislature of an extended republic (which he defended in *The Federalist No. 10*) and the Constitution's devices of checks and balances (which he vindicated in *The Federalist No. 51*) provided a solution to the problem of government abuse of power that was both theoretically satisfying and workable in practice, and on both counts more secure than formal declarations of rights could ever be. Thus, Madison at first resisted adding a declaration of rights to the Constitution at least in part because he believed that the new Federalist "science of politics" he had helped devise could perform the tasks most Americans assigned to a declaration of rights without the problems that such a declaration might cause.

A veteran drafter of constitutions and legislation, Madison understood the limitations of legal and political language—especially vague admonitory language—as a means to achieve political ends. He believed that it would be difficult, if not impossible, to draft a bill of rights that would give sufficient protection to the rights it mentioned, or that might not give protection so broad as to paralyze the needed powers of government. He also feared that it would be all too easy to leave some rights out by mistake, with the result that those rights would not be protected.

Why Madison Changed His Mind

Despite his intellectual struggles against the demand for a declaration of rights, in the summer of 1788 Madison determined to lead the effort to amend the Constitution. Four linked reasons explain his about-face, which he announced at the Virginia ratifying convention in Richmond:

• The first was the series of admonishing and persuasive letters Madison received between late 1787 and the summer of 1789 from his friend Thomas Jefferson, then American Minister to France and a keen observer of the ratification controversy. Taking pains to refute each argument that Madison raised against a declaration of rights, Jefferson reminded him that a "bill of rights is what the people are entitled to against every government on earth, general or particular, and which no government should refuse, or rest on inference." He also rebutted his younger correspondent's fears that "a positive declaration of some essential rights could not be obtained in the requisite latitude": "[H]alf a loaf is better than no bread. If we cannot secure all our rights, let us secure what we can." The Jefferson-Madison correspondence served not simply as a source of intellectual and personal leverage on Madison, but also as an indication to him that moderate Federalists throughout the nation might well think as Jefferson did. The correspondence also provided Madison with a valuable catalog of arguments that he would later use to persuade reluctant Federalist colleagues in the House and the Senate to support his amendments.

• Second, Madison's close observation of the American political scene and the communications he received from friends and political allies around the nation in 1788–1789 helped to convince him that Americans of all persuasions would rest easier if a bill of rights were added to the Constitution. Moreover, as the leader of the campaign for amend-

ments within Congress, Madison knew that he would have the most advantageous position from which to deflect any proposed amendments that might go beyond a bill of rights.
• Third, Madison feared the likelihood that diehard Anti-Federalists in New York and Virginia would make good their oft-repeated threat to seek a second general convention. If he could assume leadership of the quest for amendments within Congress, he reasoned, he might be able to deflect the momentum of the second-convention movement, or even stop it altogether. Even though only these two states' legislatures had adopted resolutions making clear their intention to demand a new convention, Virginia and New York were among the most powerful states in the Union. As the largest and most populous state (and the home state of the likely first President), Virginia wielded extraordinary political and economic power in American affairs. New York, the home of the new nation's fastest-growing port (and of its capital since 1784), was not far behind. Had Anti-Federalists in both states succeeded in making common cause against the Constitution in 1788, they might well have derailed the momentum that the Federalists had managed to build for the new charter of government. Should these two states indeed issue calls for a convention, Madison worried that other states might follow their lead—unless he placed an alternative on the agenda of Congress.

Madison feared the likelihood that diehard Anti-Federalists in New York and Virginia would make good their oft-repeated threat to seek a second generation convention.

• Fourth, and of most direct personal concern, Madison recalled the role that the demand for amendments had played during the federal elections of 1788–1789, when he ran for a seat in the first United States House of Representatives against his friend (and fellow protégé of Jefferson) James Monroe. Anti-Federalists launched a whispering campaign charging that Madison still opposed a bill of rights, despite his public pledge, which they suspected was only a ruse to lure wavering delegates to support ratification. They hoped that this charge would alienate the Baptist community, who were not only among Madison's staunchest supporters but also among the strongest advocates of a bill of rights. Madison gained election to the House largely because he refuted the charge, in person and in writing, publicly reaffirming his promises to work for the adoption of a federal bill of rights.

Thus, when the First Congress convened the following spring, Madison was already hard at work, studying with great care a pamphlet published by Augustine Davis, a Virginia printer, setting forth the more than two hundred amendments to the Constitution recommended by the ratifying conventions. Madison realized that the existence of this pamphlet and its circulation far beyond its original place of publication confirmed that the question of amendments was still alive. He therefore scoured its pages, noting redundancies and sorting out those amendments designed to identify and protect rights from those that would otherwise alter the structure of government provided by the Constitution. . . .

Madison Acts in Congress

On May 4, 1789, Madison first gave notice to his colleagues that he would act on the question of amendments, moving that the subject be raised on May 25. . . . Yet, when the appointed day for discussion of amendments arrived three weeks later, he was forced to postpone the question until June 8 to accommodate his colleagues' desire to complete work on legislation setting up federal systems of customs regulation and revenue legislation. Once again, they did not share his sense of urgency.

When June 8 came, Madison claimed recognition from the floor to fulfill his promise to his colleagues and to the nation to introduce the subject of amendments. He was confident of success, having worked hard to prepare a set of proposals that would satisfy the goals he and the President had set in Washington's inaugural address. With the people's expectations about to be gratified, and the support of the President, how could he fail?

Madison's list of proposed amendments included none that would limit the necessary powers of the general government. The Virginian aimed instead to state basic principles of republican government and to protect individual rights. Virtually every one of the twelve amendments ultimately proposed by Congress in 1789 has roots in Madison's list. He also included four provisions, derived from the Virginia Declaration of Rights and the American Declaration of Independence, affirming that government is derived from the people and is instituted to protect their liberty, safety, and happiness, and that "the people have an indubitable, unalienable, and indefeasible right to reform or change their Government, whenever it be found adverse or inadequate to the purposes of its institution." Finally, he included one other amendment not derived from any proposal, formal or informal, made during the ratification controversy: "No state shall violate the equal rights of conscience, or the freedom of the press, or the trial by jury in criminal cases."

With respect to form, Madison proposed that Congress rewrite the Constitution to incorporate the amendments in their appropriate places in the 1787 text. Thus, for example, the "bill of rights" amendments would have been added to Article I, sections 9 and 10, which limit the powers of Congress and the states. . . .

Debate over the Need for Amendments

After several postponements and a complex series of parliamentary maneuvers, the Representatives spent most of their time on June 8 squabbling over whether amendments were necessary, rather than focusing on the terms of Madison's proposal. James Jackson of Georgia argued that amendments were not needed at all, while Connecticut's Roger Sherman stressed the newness of the government authorized by the Constitution and protested that there had been nowhere near enough time to determine what, if any, defects in the system required amendment.

Madison stuck to his position, protesting, "I am sorry to be accessory to the loss of a single moment of time by the house." In defense of his motion, he made one of the greatest speeches of his career:

> If I thought I could fulfill the duty which I owe to myself and my constituents, to let the subject pass over in silence, I most certainly should not trespass upon the indulgence of this house. But I cannot do this. . . . And I do most sincerely believe that if congress will devote but one day to this subject, so far as to satisfy the public that we do not disregard their wishes, it will have a

salutary influence on the public councils, and prepare the way for a favorable reception of our future measures. It appears to me that this house is bound by every motive of prudence, not to let the first session pass over without proposing to the state legislatures some things to be incorporated into the constitution, as will render it as acceptable to the whole people of the United States, as it has been found acceptable to a majority of them.

Madison emphasized four objectives: satisfying the people of the trustworthiness of the new government, bringing the dissenting states of North Carolina and Rhode Island back into the Union, redeeming a campaign promise made by Federalists throughout the nation, and remedying a real defect in the Constitution. He then presented the amendments he thought necessary and explained and defended each in turn. It was in this speech that Madison conferred on these amendments the name, so powerful in political controversy at the time and so generally revered afterward: "The first of these amendments, related to what may be called a bill of rights." . . .

The Representatives were aware . . . of . . . the challenge of drafting a declaration of rights that would be neither too constricted nor too expansive.

On August 13, the Committee of the Whole House began its detailed debate on the proposed amendments, clause by clause, concluding on August 18. The next day, the House began formal debate, reviewing the accomplishments of the previous week. Throughout this period, Anti-Federal Representatives pleaded without avail for amendments restricting the powers of the federal judiciary and preserving state authority over congressional elections. But the House rejected these requests, as the Representatives were aware both of the need to walk a narrow line between protecting rights and damaging the powers of the government and of the challenge of drafting a declaration of rights that would be neither too constricted nor too expansive.

One key influence on the framing of the amendments

was the question whether the Constitution could permit federal intrusions into the spheres of authority of the state governments. For this reason, for example, New England Representatives persuaded Madison to recast his forthright prohibition of religious establishments to limit only the power of the federal government, thereby preventing the establishment of one or more national churches while preserving state religious establishments in New England.

Once it became clear that the House would propose amendments of some sort, the discussion shifted to the choice of words and phrases, as the Representatives groped for the right constitutional language. The major characteristic of their draftsmanship was haste. For example, what is today one of the most controversial clauses in the Bill of Rights—the Fourth Amendment's prohibition against unreasonable searches and seizures—got through with only a few minutes' debate.

The Amendments Are Not Incorporated in the Constitutional Text

It was at this point that the House, at the urging of Roger Sherman, abandoned Madison's idea of incorporating the amendments in the constitutional text. Sherman had two reasons for his demand. His first indicated his respect for the canons of legal draftsmanship:

> We ought not to interweave our propositions into the work itself, because it will be destructive of the whole fabric. We might as well endeavor to mix brass, iron, and clay, as to incorporate such heterogeneous articles; the one contradictory to the other. Its absurdity will be discovered by comparing it with a law: would any legislature endeavor to introduce into a former act, a subsequent amendment, and let them stand so connected. When an alteration is made in an act, it is done by way of supplement; the latter act always repealing the former in every specified case of difference.

His second reason, one of principle, was grounded in his understanding of the Constitution as an exercise of the constituent power by the People of the United States through their delegates in the Federal Convention:

> The constitution is the act of the people, and ought to

remain entire. But the amendments will be the act of the state governments; again all the authority we possess, is derived from that instrument [the Constitution]; if we mean to destroy the whole and establish a new constitution, we remove the basis on which we mean to build.

Despite the resistance of Madison and some of his colleagues, the House adopted Sherman's point of view. This vote set a precedent for all future exercises of the amending power. The House's decision, setting amendments aside from the rest of the Constitution, would lead to the placement of the Bill of Rights at the head of the post–1787 text of the document, thus ensuring its primacy in popular imagination.

On August 24, the House endorsed the seventeen draft amendments, but once the amendments made their way up the stairs of Federal Hall to the Senate the next morning, our detailed knowledge of the debates evaporates. Unlike the House, which had a visitors' gallery and several self-employed reporters recording the proceedings, the Senate met behind closed doors. The only record of its actions appears in its bare-bones Legislative and Executive Journals, which record motions and votes but not debates or individual speeches.

Role of the Senate

What we do know is that the Senate, containing only two Anti-Federalists out of twenty-two members, was much less responsive to the desirability of amendments than the House, which, despite its Federalist majority, had a significantly high proportion of Anti-Federal members from key states such as Virginia, New York, Massachusetts, and South Carolina. The amendments produced by the Senate on September 9 dramatized the Senators' coolness. The Senate reduced the House's proposals from seventeen to twelve and significantly weakened them. For example, the House version of the religious-liberty provision clearly deprived Congress of any power over religion:

> Congress shall make no law establishing religion or prohibiting the free exercise thereof, nor shall the rights of Conscience be infringed.

By contrast, the Senate's version only barred Congress from creating an established church like the Church of England:

> Congress shall make no law establishing articles of faith, or a mode of worship, or prohibiting the free exercise of religion.

Although Roger Sherman declared that, in his view, the amendments had been "altered for the Better," Madison was angered by the Senate's handiwork. . . .

A "conference committee" of three Representatives and three Senators—the usual method of resolving an impasse between the chambers of a bicameral legislature—restored many of the twelve proposed amendments to the form favored by the House; the House approved the final list of twelve on September 24, 1789, and the Senate concurred in two votes on September 25 and 26. . . .

The States Ratify the Bill of Rights

Anti-Federalists divided over the Amendments proposed by Congress. Some, who had objected to the Constitution because it lacked a declaration of rights, welcomed the Amendments and abandoned their distrust of the new government. Others, who wanted to restrict the general government's powers over taxation and regulation of interstate and foreign commerce, charged that the Amendments produced by Congress only distracted the people from the serious flaws still present in the Constitution. Federalists rejected these arguments with scorn, pointing out that those who had painted themselves as friends of liberty now showed their true colors by opposing the Bill of Rights.

The ratification process started quickly; several states adopted the Amendments almost as soon as the engrossed copies arrived. Among these was North Carolina, one of the two holdout states. Its legislature ratified the Amendments on December 22, 1789, one month after its second ratifying convention had adopted the Constitution (194 to 77). Rhode Island was more stubborn. It took veiled threats of trade reprisals from Congress, the refusal of President Washington to visit the state during his fall 1789 tour of New England, and secession talk from the Federalists of Providence and Newport before the state at last called a ratifying convention to assemble in April 1790. The convention took nearly a month to adopt the Constitution by a two-vote margin (34 to 32), with dozens of recommended amendments; less than two weeks later, on June 11, the Rhode Island legislature adopted the Bill of Rights.

Anti-Federalists in the Virginia legislature were bitterly disappointed by the Amendments, because they included none reining in the powers of the general government over taxation and commerce. Following the lead of their commander, Patrick Henry, they blocked action in the legislature's upper house for months.

By March 4, 1791, nine states had ratified ten of the twelve proposed Amendments, leaving them one state short of the required three-fourths. On that date, Vermont joined the Union. The problem was that, with Vermont's addition to the Union (and even after its ratification of the Amendments on November 3), the number of necessary state ratifications automatically rose from ten (out of thirteen) to eleven (out of fourteen). With no word from Connecticut, Massachusetts, or Georgia, the focus shifted back to Virginia. Supporters of the Amendments in the Virginia legislature revived them, mocking the diehard Anti-Federalists as obstacles to the amendments they had demanded years before; caught in an uncomfortable political predicament, the Anti-Federalists at last gave in to overwhelming pressure. On December 15, 1791, Virginia ratified all but the first of the twelve proposed amendments and added the third through the twelfth to the Constitution as the Bill of Rights.

Chapter 2

The Bill of Rights over the Years

1

The Original Bill of Rights Was Flawed

Ira Glasser

Ira Glasser was the executive director of the American Civil Liberties Union from 1978 to 2001. In the selection below, he cites several problems with the Bill of Rights. He notes that the biggest problem was its failure to protect citizens from abuses of power perpetrated by state governments. In addition, entire groups of people were left out of the promised liberties—women, American Indians, and African Americans. Correcting these flaws in the Bill of Rights has been a long, slow process.

Although it was a grand statement of lofty legal principles, the original Bill of Rights contained several glaring, nearly fatal flaws.

The Biggest Problem with the Bill of Rights

First, and most importantly, it did not apply to state governments. The First Amendment, for example, prohibited *Congress* from abridging the right to free speech or freedom of the press, but it didn't prohibit any state—or, for that matter, local—government from censoring speech or banning newspapers or restricting the freedom of religion. James Madison's proposed amendment prohibiting states from violating certain fundamental rights, such as freedom of the press and religion and the right to trial by jury, was the only amendment rejected by the Senate. As a result, state governments were left unrestricted, free to violate individual rights as they pleased. They could imprison people

Excerpted from *Visions of Liberty*, by Ira Glasser (New York: Arcade Publishing, 1991). Copyright © 1991 by Ira Glasser. Reprinted with permission.

for their religious or political beliefs, abolish trial by jury, even torture suspects to extort confessions. However grand the Bill of Rights sounded, at the outset it provided no legal protection against the states.

This was a major flaw, to put it mildly, since most government activity affecting the lives of ordinary people was carried out by state and local governments. That was where people lived. To lack protection against state and local government was to be without rights. That is why Madison called his proposed amendment "the most valuable" of all.

An Early Court Decision

In 1833, a man named John Barron tried to use the Bill of Rights in a dispute he had with the city of Baltimore. The city had seized some of Barron's property, and he claimed that under the Fifth Amendment he was entitled to "just compensation." The Fifth Amendment did in fact appear to support his claim, since it prohibited the government from taking "private property . . . for public use, without just compensation." But the Supreme Court ruled that the Fifth Amendment, and indeed the entire Bill of Rights, applied only to the federal government, not to state or local governments.

That the Supreme Court hardly ever used its power to protect individual rights during the early years of our nation's history should thus come as no surprise. Most often, rights were violated by state and local governments, and they were completely immune from the legal restraints in the Bill of Rights. It would take a civil war to change the situation.

Amendments After the Civil War

In 1868, the Fourteenth Amendment was passed; it was one of three constitutional amendments passed after the Civil War to address the rights of the newly freed slaves. The Thirteenth Amendment permanently prohibited "slavery and involuntary servitude" and gave Congress the power to enforce that prohibition through legislation. The Fifteenth Amendment forbade both federal *and* state governments from abridging the right to vote "on account of race, color, or previous condition of servitude"; it, too, gave Congress the power of enforcement.

But the Fourteenth Amendment was more complex and far-reaching. It provided, in part, that

No state shall . . . abridge the privileges or immunities of citizens of the United States; nor shall any state deprive any person of life, liberty, or property without due process of law; nor deny to any person within its jurisdiction the equal protection of the laws.

Most often, rights were violated by state and local governments. . . . It would take a civil war to change the situation.

This language appears to be a more general form of Madison's rejected amendment and would seem to mean that no state can legally violate the rights of its citizens, including the rights guaranteed by the Bill of Rights. Indeed, some historians and some Supreme Court justices believe that the Fourteenth Amendment was explicitly intended by its authors to overrule *Barron v. Baltimore*. Other historians disagree, and think the historical record is "probably inconclusive." But ultimately any constitutional provision means what the Supreme Court says it means, and for a long time the Court ruled that the Fourteenth Amendment did *not* apply the Bill of Rights to the states.

A Key Decision Negates the Fourteenth Amendment

In 1873, five years after the Fourteenth Amendment was adopted, the Supreme Court rendered its first decision interpreting its meaning. The case grew out of a commercial controversy that seemed at first to have very little to do with the lives of most Americans. In 1869, the state of Louisiana, through its licensing power, had granted a monopoly on butchering to a single company, the Crescent City Stock Landing and Slaughterhouse Company. Butchers who were excluded claimed discrimination and a deprivation of their livelihood, and argued that Louisiana's actions violated the second clause of the new Fourteenth Amendment, which prohibited states from abridging the rights (or, in the language of the amendment, the "privileges and immunities") of United States citizens.

The Supreme Court ruled that the Fourteenth Amendment did not apply. Though it did clearly prohibit states from violating the rights of United States citizens, the Court ruled that the "privileges and immunities" of United States citizens did not include the full range of individual liberties set forth in the Bill of Rights. Instead, the Court ruled that the only rights protected by the "privileges and immunities" clause of the Fourteenth Amendment were rights of *national* citizenship, such as the right to travel or the right to go to Washington and petition the *national* government.

By settling a commercial dispute between butchers and the state of Louisiana the way it did, the Supreme Court in effect nullified the capacity of the Fourteenth Amendment to correct the restrictive interpretation of the Bill of Rights rendered by the Court's 1833 decision in *Barron v. Baltimore*. Therefore, despite the Fourteenth Amendment, the Bill of Rights still provided no protection in the circumstances where it was most needed.

It took another half-century before the Court began to use the other clauses of the Fourteenth Amendment to apply the Bill of Rights to state and local governments. But it would be a slow process. Not until the 1960s—nearly a century after the Fourteenth Amendment was passed—would the Bill of Rights be applied comprehensively to the states. A narrow commercial dispute turned out to diminish the rights of tens of millions of Americans for almost a hundred years.

Women and American Indians Left Out

The failure to apply any part of the Bill of Rights to the states was a serious omission in 1791, but it wasn't the only omission. At its inception, the Bill of Rights was not intended to protect everyone. Whole groups of people were left out. Women were seen as second-class citizens, at best. The prevailing social view was that women were the property of their husbands, and this was in part reflected in the new Constitution. The very language of our early declarations of principles was exclusionary. When in the Declaration of Independence the principle of equality was announced, by its own terms it was exclusionary: "All *men* are created equal," it said. In a system designed grandly to ensure people the right to have a say, through elections, in how they would be governed, women were not even entitled to vote.

The right to vote, of course, derived in large part from property qualifications. "All men are created equal" excluded more than just women: it also excluded most men.

The consent of the governed was commonly understood to be limited to the consent of property owners. Later, property qualifications for voting were abandoned, often to be replaced by taxpayer qualifications. In time, many of these were abandoned as well. But even after such tests were abolished, women continued to be denied the vote. The Bill of Rights was in force for nearly 130 years before the right of women to vote was recognized and guaranteed by the Nineteenth Amendment.

The group most grievously excluded from the protections of the original Bill of Rights were African slaves and their descendants.

If women were partially unprotected by the original Constitution, others were completely unprotected. American Indians, for example, were entirely outside the constitutional system, since they were defined by the United States as an alien people within their own land, decimated, militarily defeated, and confined to reservations. They were not American citizens, and thus were governed, not by ordinary American laws, but by federal treaties and statutes that stripped tribes of most of their land and much of their authority. In 1924, Congress belatedly granted all Indians United States citizenship, but it has never completely resolved the issue of tribal sovereignty. To this day, the degree to which individual Americans of Indian descent are protected by the Bill of Rights against the powers of *tribal* governments remains ambiguous.

African Slaves and Their Descendants Left Out

But the group most grievously excluded from the protections of the original Bill of Rights were African slaves and their descendants. Their exclusion was not inadvertent, and it indelibly stained the Constitution and the ideals of liberty it claimed to protect and symbolize.

By the time of the Revolution in 1776, slavery was nearly universally believed to be "the absolute political evil." It is not difficult to see why. The philosophical force driving the fight for freedom from English rule was the belief that individual rights were God-given *to every human being;* that the attainment of liberty was the highest social good; and that the mortal enemy of liberty was unlimited power, the *dominion* of some people over others. The most propulsive political force at the time was the idea that power must be sharply limited. The polar opposite of sharply limited power was *slavery*, what one pamphleteer defined as "being wholly under the power and control of another," and what a newspaper writer in 1747 described as "a force . . . by which a man is obliged to act, or not to act, according to the arbitrary will and pleasure of another." Thus defined, slavery represented the death of liberty, the end result of the failure to limit power. . . .

In the end, [slavery] was tolerated. Thomas Jefferson wrote that "the abolition of domestic slavery is the great object of desire," but he owned slaves himself and took no serious steps to outlaw the slave trade even when he was president. Patrick Henry, the fiery Anti-Federalist who refused to accept the original Constitution without a bill of rights, wrote that he looked forward to a time "when an opportunity will be offered to abolish this lamentable evil." But that time would have to wait because, Henry said, "the general inconvenience of living here without them" made freeing the slaves impractical.

And so the great apostles of liberty came to tolerate the greatest possible denial of liberty in their midst. Believing that they could not both abolish slavery *and* form a strong Union, they accepted political reality. . . .

The general principles of liberty and equality upon which the Constitution was based did . . . provide some impetus years later to extend the Bill of Rights to those initially excluded. The contradictions between the ideals expressed by the Bill of Rights and the realities of American life have been steadily, if slowly and unevenly, resolved in favor of the ideals.

2

The Blessings of Liberty

Aric Press

Aric Press is editorial director of the American Lawyer Media's national publications and editor-in-chief of *American Lawyer* magazine. In the following selection he focuses on the "rights revolution," as he calls it, during which federal judges began to challenge the power of state legislatures in order to protect the freedoms listed in the Bill of Rights. He explains that although the Constitution is more than 200 years old, constitutional rights are only about 50 years old. That, he argues, is because in the early years of the Constitution, each individual state set its own limits on the rights of its citizens. Then, in the 1920s, a power shift occurred during which the judicial branch of the federal government began citing the Fourteenth Amendment and its attendant guarantees of "due process" and "equal protection" of the laws. In the landmark *Gitlow* case of 1925, a guarantee in the Bill of Rights—freedom of speech—was for the first time seen to be protected from state intervention. That ushered in a new era of judicial review, in effect a "rights revolution" that has been going on for the past half century.

The real American anthem: I know my rights. All Americans know that the Constitution puts limits on what government can do to them. What most do not realize is that while the Constitution itself is 200 years old, as a practical matter most constitutional *rights* date back no more than a half century. For much of our history, each state decided for itself the limits it would place on free speech or racial equality. It was only in the 1920s that federal judges began transforming the Constitution into gen-

From "The Blessings of Liberty," by Aric Press, *Newsweek*, May 25, 1987. Copyright © 1987 by *Newsweek*. Reprinted with permission.

uinely supreme law. "We were always a free country," says University of Virginia historian Henry J. Abraham, "but in the past the freedom was often hypothetical."

The rights revolution was accomplished by one of the great power shifts in the federal government's history. On issues of civil rights and liberties, federal judges dropped their deference to legislatures and became an independent force to be reckoned with. "The emergence of judge-made constitutional law has been the most striking characteristic of our federal courts since the end of the nineteenth century," writes political scientist Christopher Wolfe of Marquette University. That development has not been universally applauded. Some critics complain about the tyranny of unelected judges. Others strongly disagree with the substance of the court's work: rulings on abortion or prayer in schools draw fire that muffles the cool, academic debates over judicial review.

Most of the individual liberties guaranteed by the Constitution are included in the first 10 amendments, the Bill of Rights, which was ratified in 1791. Like so much of the framers' work, they were the product of a deal: during the fight for ratification, many anti-federalists—opponents of strong central government—demanded a bill of rights as the price of support for the Constitution. The language is spare yet ringing: guaranteeing, for example, freedom of speech and religion against congressional infringement; prohibitions against warrantless searches and self-incrimination, and the right to a speedy trial. But the Bill of Rights had a built-in flaw: it did not protect citizens against encroachments by state governments. Nor was this loophole ever questioned by the first members of the Supreme Court, men who knew at first hand the intent of the framers.

Then came the supreme constitutional reform—the Civil War. After Appomattox, the Radical Republicans who controlled Congress drafted constitutional amendments that the Southern states would have to approve before they could rejoin the Union. Two were clear: the 13th barred slavery and the 15th prohibited states from interfering with the right to vote (except for women). But the 14th was open ended, barring *states* from denying "any person" either "due process" or "equal protection" of law. Adopted in 1868, that language had no legal meaning for more than a half century. It was when courts breathed life into those words that the individual-rights revolution began. And the result, according to political scientist Richard C. Corner of the University of Arizona, was "our second bill of rights, a bill more salient to the liberty of the average American than the original document."

Seditious pamphlet: The first stirrings came over free speech and political protest. Early in the century several states passed laws against advocating the overthrow of the government; other statutes sought to bar protests against the first world war. As prosecutions mounted—three New York men were charged with distributing a seditious pamphlet that included the text of the First Amendment—appeals reached the U.S. Supreme Court. Initially, only Justices Louis Brandeis and Oliver Wendell Holmes objected to these curbs on free speech; for the others, the Bill of Rights simply did not apply to the states. That rule changed in 1925: Benjamin Gitlow, a radical Socialist, was convicted in New York of advocating the "overthrow of the government" by force or violence. In one of the most famous civil-liberties decisions, a split high court upheld Gitlow's conviction. But, for the first time, the justices also declared that the due-process clause of the 14th Amendment, declaring that no state shall "deprive any person of life, liberty or property without due process of law," protected freedom of speech from state "impairment."

Broad expansion: The victory was little comfort to Gitlow, who served three years in prison (and later finished his political career as a government informer). But it was vital to the course of civil liberties. In legalese, the Gitlow case began the process of "incorporating" the Bill of Rights into the 14th Amendment. Finally, the federal courts were taking civil liberties seriously.

It was the beginning of a broad expansion of judicial authority. In its first brush with the rights of defendants, the court held that at a minimum the Sixth Amendment guaranteed a lawyer to an indigent charged with a capital crime. The case involved the famous Scottsboro boys of Alabama: seven poor, young black men falsely charged with raping two white women. The court held that convicting them after a one-day trial in which they had no legal representation violated "those fundamental principles of liberty and justice which lie at the base of all our civil and political institutions." Though "fundamental," this principle was not upheld until 1932. And the right to counsel in noncapital felonies came even later, in 1963.

In the 1930s, of course, the Supreme Court's main concerns lay elsewhere, with New Deal economic legislation. Repeatedly the court struck down these laws as infringements on due process—"a massive and unprecedented judicial assault on a single administration," wrote legal historian Leonard W. Levy. During one 17-month period in 1935–36, the justices voided 12 acts of Congress. The rulings provoked Franklin D. Roosevelt into a controversial campaign to expand the court's membership and "pack" it with his loyalists. The practical problem for the high court, then, was to find a way to move in two directions at once: expand its reach in civil rights yet end its conflict with the New Deal on economic issues. According to Harvard law professor Archibald Cox, the court found "the logical escape." In 1937 Justice Benjamin Cardozo established an "honor roll of superior rights" representing the "very essence of a scheme of ordered liberty." These rights included free speech, fair trials and the free practice of religion. The next year Justice Harlan Fiske Stone completed the escape by announcing a new double standard of legislation: laws that touched on basic liberties or racial minorities would be given "strict scrutiny" by the courts; economic legislation would not.

The court continued "incorporating" the Bill of Rights for the next three decades, but always in a selective manner. Some provisions have never been formally incorporated against the states, most notably the constitutional right to bear arms. As incorporation became an accepted legal tool—although one still heatedly debated by a small group of scholars—the court's docket filled with issues touching on the 14th Amendment guarantee of "equal protection of the laws." Those cases, according to New York University law professor John Sexton, "transformed equality from a nebulous goal into a pivotal doctrine of American constitutional law."

But not overnight. It wasn't until 1954 that the Supreme Court struck down the system of "separate but equal" segregated schools in the landmark case of *Brown v. Board of Education*. Once begun, equal-protection jurisprudence became the high court's engine of social reform. In the name of equal protection the justices enshrined one man, one vote as a constitutional principle in reapportionment cases. They applied the concept to laws adversely affecting women, illegitimate children and aliens. They even used it to create special fundamental rights—such as the freedom to marry someone of a different race.

Hard language: This judicial surge produced an inevitable backlash. Under the colors of judicial review, had the court become, in the words of Justice Brandeis, a "superlegislature?" Whatever the merits of individual policy decisions, critics demanded, who elected the justices? And, as they moved further from the hard language of the Constitution, just what were they relying on—if not the document itself? Perhaps the most controversial example of judicial innovation was the abortion decision of 1973, *Roe v. Wade*. There, the court peered into the "penumbras" of various constitutional provisions and discerned a woman's right, within certain limits, to terminate a pregnancy. Despite objections that unelected and therefore unaccountable agencies should leave politically divisive questions for politicians to settle, *Roe* remains the law of the land; it was reaffirmed just last year [1986].

Even if it were desirable, the habit of relying on the courts would be hard to break. The elected branches are all too content to pass the tough questions on to the bench: federal judges, after all, have lifetime appointments. In any event, courts react more than they lead—a fact obscured by the current focus on judicial policymaking. As Stanford University legal historian Lawrence M. Friedman points out, judges do not work in a vacuum: "The 'due process revolution' is the product of social change." Citizens must assert a right before a court has occasion to endorse it. Do free institutions create a free people? Or is it the other way around?

We may now be at a legal and political watershed. It has been a remarkable half century, but except for privacy issues such as those arising from breakthroughs in surveillance technology, what new rights are left for the courts to recognize? Our leading domestic problems—jobs, education, housing, families, safety—do not seem to lend themselves to ready judicial fiat. Their place on the public agenda is for the most part in candidates' position papers, not on court dockets. To be sure, they will all eventually become legal issues; everything does in America, as Tocqueville reported 150 years ago. But the next phase of the rights revolution must begin in the political arena—a place the Founding Fathers always found comfortable.

3

The Bill of Rights Has Led to Excessive Demands for Rights

Charlotte Low

Charlotte Low (Allen), author of *The Human Christ*, has written articles for the *Atlantic Monthly*, the *New York Times*, the *Washington Post*, the *Wall Street Journal*, and other major publications. She was contributing editor for *Lingua Franca*, a magazine about intellectual and literary life in the academy, and senior editor for *Crisis* magazine. In the selection below, she relates that the Bill of Rights was virtually unused for more than one hundred years after its addition to the Constitution. A crucial decision in 1925 by the Supreme Court allowed state laws to be struck down if they violated any of the first ten amendments to the Constitution. Low argues that as a result, Americans have been eagerly trying to establish an increasing number of individual and group rights, with the result that the rights of some groups have begun to infringe on those of others.

Everyone has, or claims, rights—the accused criminal, the accused criminal's putative victim, the tenant, the landlord, the divorced father, the divorced mother, the surrogate mother, the welfare mother, the fired employee, the prison newspaper editor, the stranded air traveler. . . .

In California, several years ago, a man won the right to wear a leisure suit at a restaurant with a coat-and-tie rule; the court said the rule was unfair because it did not apply to women. Ladies Day at the car wash has bitten the dust in

Excerpted from "Someone's Rights, Another's Wrongs," by Charlotte Low, *Insight*, January 26, 1987. Copyright © 1987 by *Insight*. Reprinted with permission.

several states on discrimination grounds. A group of fathers in New York recently won a settlement establishing a nursery area in an airport men's room so they can change babies' diapers as women do.

"The Founding Fathers would roll over in their graves if they knew how the protections they devised for honest people have been used by those on the fringe—violent criminals, pornographers, rapists, even people who have renounced their citizenship," says Daniel Popeo, founder of the conservative Washington Legal Foundation and archcritic of the rights explosion.

Origin of the Bill of Rights

The Bill of Rights, as the Constitution's first 10 amendments are known, was not part of the document signed at Philadelphia on Sept. 17, 1787. Indeed, Alexander Hamilton devoted several Federalist Papers to arguing that the amendments were unnecessary because the body of the Constitution contained a wide variety of protections for citizens, including guaranteed jury trials and bans on arbitrary imprisonment.

It was not that the Founding Fathers lacked a sense of individual rights, points out Walter Berns, a legal theorist at the American Enterprise Institute. But the founders, says Berns, "viewed the idea of separation of powers and representative government as the fundamental way of securing those rights."

The Dormant Bill of Rights

Nonetheless, at the insistence of several state legislatures, Congress quickly added the Bill of Rights to the Constitution in 1789. There it lay, virtually dormant, for more than a century. Between 1789 and 1925, the Supreme Court used the first 10 amendments to outlaw government acts in only 15 cases, Berns counts. Just nine cases involving Bill of Rights issues were decided during the entire 19th century, one of them the infamous Dred Scott ruling that slaves were not citizens and could not sue for their freedom in federal court.

One reason for the paucity of rulings was that "there's not much there" in the Bill of Rights, as Professor Lino Graglia of the University of Texas's law school puts it. Except for guarantees of free speech, press and religion in the First Amendment, most of the rights involve details of criminal procedure. The Espionage Act of 1917, a sweeping ban on agitation against mobilization for World War I, prompted the court to pay some attention to the First Amendment during the early part of this century, and the invention of bugging technology prompted a few search and seizure rulings.

"Incorporation"

Then two things happened. One was the development of the doctrine of "incorporation." After the Civil War, with the goal of overturning the Dred Scott ruling, the 14th Amendment was added to the Constitution, guaranteeing rights of citizenship and equal protection of the law to all races. It also forbade states to deprive "any person of life, liberty and property without due process of law." Starting with a 1925 decision, the Supreme Court began to interpret that due process guarantee as incorporating most provisions of the Bill of Rights.

This meant, for the first time, that a state law could be struck down as violating the First, the Fourth, the Fifth Amendment and so forth. Although conservative legal analysts, including Attorney General Edwin Meese III, decry the incorporation doctrine—allowing Supreme Court review of state as well as federal legislation—as a wholly artificial development and a federal club against the states, scholars generally agree it is here to stay after more than 60 years.

Civil Rights

The second development, almost contemporaneous with incorporation, was a determined campaign by the National Association for the Advancement of Colored People and similar groups to put teeth into post–Civil War civil rights guarantees. Racially segregated school systems prevailed in the South and elsewhere; Jim Crow laws and local customs kept blacks out of white hotels, restaurants, rest rooms and polling places. But in 1954, NAACP-allied lawyers won a major victory: *Brown vs. Board of Education*, striking down a segregated school system in Topeka, Kan., as a violation of equal protection.

The Brown ruling marked the beginning of the end of legal segregation in the United States. (The real end did not come, many observers say, until Congress passed tough laws during the 1960s forbidding discrimination in hiring, voting and housing.) But it also marked the beginning, says

Graglia, of a determined meliorism on the part of such key justices of the time as Earl Warren, William O. Douglas and William Brennan Jr. . . . —a notion that constitutional law could solve widespread social ills as well as resolve individual grievances. "It was a very popular notion during the 1950s," says Graglia, "that people are infinitely malleable."

Criminal Issues

On criminal issues, Graglia says, the notion became "There but for the grace of God go I." During the 1950s, 1960s and early 1970s, criminal procedural rights blossomed as in a desert spring. The Supreme Court extended the exclusionary rule—a rule the federal courts had developed barring illegally seized evidence from criminal trials—to all state criminal cases. It outlined a series of "Miranda" warnings about the consequences of incriminating statements that accused criminals must receive before they confess.

Death penalty laws were struck down, jury selections scrutinized. Even state prison conditions became subject to federal court monitoring. The new rules keep police and prosecutors honest, supporters say. But the net result has been detailed federal court supervision of even the tiniest aspects of state and local procedures.

Other Groups with Grievances

Meanwhile, other groups with grievances were inspired by the success of blacks. "The idea of equality, once loosed, had to grow," says Dennis Hutchinson, a constitutional historian at the University of Chicago. "Once the thrust of society becomes egalitarian, everyone wants a share. You have civil rights for the handicapped, the mentally retarded and so on. The natural end of this, of course, is that groups start fighting each other."

The Supreme Court, obliging, has created special niches of protection for some of the groups that have appeared before it. Women, at 51 percent of the population, cannot claim the specially protected status of racial minorities, so the court has given them a hybrid "third-tier" level of constitutional protection, somewhere between racial groups and ordinary male citizens. Welfare recipients and other beneficiaries of public funds now have a right to hearings before their benefits are terminated, thanks to a 1970 Supreme Court ruling that the benefits are a form of property.

Congress and state legislatures have also stepped into the rights ring. During the past 20 years, women, the handicapped and the elderly have secured laws protecting them from discrimination in employment, credit and educational opportunities. Wisconsin and 56 cities now have laws barring discrimination against homosexuals, although homosexuals have been singularly unsuccessful in a 10-year effort to persuade Congress to include them in federal civil rights laws.

Conflicts Among Those Seeking Rights

As Hutchinson notes, the proliferation of rights has caused conflicts among rights claimants. The most serious example of this probably has been the battle over affirmative action, the notion of preferential hirings, promotions and places in professional schools for minority group members and, sometimes, women. The equal treatment language of the 14th Amendment specifies only that everyone is entitled to equal protection of the law, and members of Congress specifically disavowed the idea of racial quotas when they passed a comprehensive job discrimination ban in 1964. Nonetheless, activist lawyers and courts, along with employers seeking to mitigate racial strife, have tended to interpret the equal treatment guarantees as providing comprehensive future remedies for groups claiming past discrimination.

The Brown ruling marked the beginning of . . . a notion that constitutional law could solve widespread social ills.

The effect has been to pit innocent groups—minority group members and women looking for jobs and promotions vs. white men who had never indulged in discrimination themselves—against each other in a high-stakes, zero-sum game. The Supreme Court has tried to trim back affirmative action somewhat. In several decisions it has struck down plans that required layoffs of higher-seniority whites so lower-seniority blacks could keep their jobs. But generally, the court has allowed the plans to stay in place, rejecting the claims of white men. . . .

Attempts to avoid promoting religion—banning it from public school textbooks—generate claims of interference with religious freedom. Crime victims complain that courts ignore their rights while affecting solicitude over those of criminals; California now has a "Victim's Bill of Rights" tightening procedural rules.

Right to Privacy Controversy

All these conflicts pale, however, beside the controversy over the Supreme Court's discovery—or creation—of a "fundamental" right to privacy. The right made its first full-fledged appearance in a 1965 decision, *Griswold vs. Connecticut*, striking down a Connecticut law banning the sale of birth control devices, even to married couples. The opinion by William O. Douglas rested on notions of the sanctity of marriage; he called it a "right of privacy older than the Bill of Rights." A few years later, however, the court was approving contraceptive sales to the unmarried and teenagers.

On the reproductive front, the Griswold ruling led straight to *Roe vs. Wade* in 1973, establishing a woman's right to have an abortion, over claims that abortion has little to do with marital intimacy On other fronts, the idea of privacy evolved under the aegis of the courts into the right of high school students to wear their hair long, the nondangerous mentally ill to wander homeless on the streets and transvestites to cross-dress, as long as it was in psychological preparation for a sex change operation.

The proliferation of rights has caused conflicts among rights claimants.

The Supreme Court balked at recognizing a privacy right for homosexual sodomy, deciding it would be "facetious" to imagine such acts were enshrined in the Constitution. But one commentator, *New Republic* Editor Michael Kinsley, humorously wondered why the court chose to draw the line at sodomy when it granted constitutional protection to just about every other form of sexual activity.

In all seriousness, the Supreme Court struggled with issues such as family privacy long before the current rights mania, and the question of whether the Constitution should reflect a higher moral law is one that has plagued scholars for decades. In the early part of the twentieth century, the court invoked vague notions of marriage and family rights to strike down laws requiring sterilization of felons and forbidding parents to send their children to parochial schools. "The general public has simply taken those rights for granted," says Laurence Tribe, a professor of constitutional law at Harvard University. Tribe discounts the controversy over the rights explosion as really a controversy over specific and unpopular rights and remedies the court has recognized: abortion, busing and affirmative action.

Why We Are Preoccupied with Rights

Meanwhile, the shouting and the arm wrestling, the struggle of "all against all," as Thomas Hobbes called it, is likely to continue in the legal arena as Americans translate their desires and their grievances into notions of rights. "There's an idea current among the general public that no one should ever have to suffer the slightest hardship, that the teeniest nick in one's sensibilities creates a right, that you should never force anyone to do anything," says Bruce Fein, a former Reagan administration counsel and constitutional scholar at the Heritage Foundation.

Fein, like some other observers, traces the current preoccupation with rights to a decline in the family, religion and other institutions that inspire individuals to transcend their own concerns. "It used to be thought that people should be able to live with hardship, that necessity was the mother of invention. But now it's just a matter of who's screaming the loudest in court. The mental stress of the mother outweighs the claims of the tiny handicapped infant, even when you offer to take it off her hands, put it up for adoption."

Are we becoming a nation of whiners? In 1840, Alexis de Tocqueville wrote in "Democracy in America" that such may be the inevitable fate of atomistic, democratic man. "Thus not only does democracy make every man forget his ancestors but hides his descendants and separates his contemporaries from him; it throws him back forever upon himself alone and threatens in the end to confine him entirely within the solitude of his heart." This grim assessment may be truer than ever.

4

The Bill of Rights Is the Best Hope for Freedom

Hugo Black

Hugo Black was an associate justice of the Supreme Court from 1937 to 1971. He became noted for his defense of First Amendment rights. In the following selection, taken from the first James Madison Lecture at New York University School of Law in 1960, Black praises the uniqueness of the Constitution and the Bill of Rights. Unlike previous bills of rights, the American one denied or tightly restricted the powers of government. He gives examples of English and early American abuses of governmental powers and explains that the Americans demanded a bill of rights for protection against political and religious persecution. Black believes the Constitution with the Bill of Rights does a good job balancing conflicting interests. He says these two documents are the best hope for freedom today; they are not outdated.

W hat is a bill of rights? In the popular sense it is any document setting forth the liberties of the people. I prefer to think of our Bill of Rights as including all provisions of the original Constitution and Amendments that protect individual liberty by barring government from acting in a particular area or from acting except under certain prescribed procedures. I have in mind such clauses in the body of the Constitution itself as those which safeguard the right of habeas corpus, forbid bills of attainder and ex post facto laws, guarantee trial by jury, and strictly define treason and limit the way it can be tried and punished. I would cer-

Excerpted from Hugo Black's lecture at the New York University School of Law, February 17, 1960.

tainly add to this list the last constitutional prohibition in Article Six that "no religious Test shall ever be required as a Qualification to any Office or public Trust under the United States."

The Americans who supported the Revolution and the adoption of our Constitution knew firsthand the dangers of tyrannical governments.

I shall speak to you about the Bill of Rights only as it bears on powers of the Federal Government. Originally, the first ten amendments were not intended to apply to the states but, as the Supreme Court held in 1833 in *Barron v. Baltimore*, were adopted to quiet fears extensively entertained that the powers of the big new national government "might be exercised in a manner dangerous to liberty." I believe that by virtue of the Fourteenth Amendment, the first ten amendments are now applicable to the state, a view I stated in *Adamson v. California*. I adhere to that view. In this talk, however, I want to discuss only the extent to which the Bill of Rights limits the Federal Government. . . .

The Uniqueness of Our Bill of Rights

It is my belief that there are "absolutes" in our Bill of Rights, and that they were put there on purpose by men who knew what words meant, and meant their prohibitions to be "absolutes." The whole history and background of the Constitution and Bill of Rights, as I understand it, belies the assumption or conclusion that our ultimate constitutional freedoms are no more than our English ancestors had when they came to this new land to get new freedoms. The historical and practical purposes of a Bill of Rights, the very use of a written constitution, indigenous to America, the language the Framers used, the kind of three-department government they took pains to set up, all point to the creation of a government which was denied all power to do some things under any and all circumstances, and all power to do other things except precisely in the manner prescribed. . . . I am primarily discussing here whether liberties admittedly covered by the Bill of Rights can nevertheless be abridged on

the ground that a superior public interest justifies the abridg-
ment. I think the Bill of Rights made its safeguards superior.

Today most Americans seem to have forgotten the ancient evils which forced their ancestors to flee to this new
country and to form a government stripped of old powers
used to oppress them. But the Americans who supported the
Revolution and the adoption of our Constitution knew firsthand the dangers of tyrannical governments. They were familiar with the long existing practice of English persecu-
tions of people wholly because of their religious or political
beliefs. They knew that many accused of such offenses had
stood, helpless to defend themselves, before biased legislators and judges. . . .

Unfortunately, our own colonial history provided ample
reasons for people to be afraid to vest too much power in
the national government. There had been bills of attainder
here; women had been convicted and sentenced to death as
"witches"; Quakers, Baptists, and various Protestant sects
had been persecuted from time to time. Roger Williams left
Massachusetts to breathe the free air of new Rhode Island.
Catholics were barred from holding office in many places.
Test oaths were required in some of the colonies to bar any
but "Christians" from holding office. In New England
Quakers suffered death for their faith. Baptists were sent to
jail in Virginia for preaching, which caused Madison, while
a very young man, to deplore what he called that "diaboli-
cal hell-conceived principle of persecution."

---

*I believe that our Constitution, with its absolute
guarantees of individual rights, is the best hope
for the aspirations of freedom which men share
everywhere.*

In the light of history, therefore, it is not surprising that
when our Constitution was adopted without specific provisions to safeguard cherished individual rights from invasion
by the legislative, as well as the executive and judicial de-
partments of the National Government, a loud and irre-
sistible clamor went up throughout the country. These
protests were so strong that the Constitution was ratified by
the very narrowest of votes in some of the states. It has been

said, and I think correctly, that had there been no general agreement that a supplementary Bill of Rights would be adopted as soon as possible after Congress met, the Constitution would not have been ratified. It seems clear that this widespread demand for a Bill of Rights was due to a common fear of political and religious persecution should the national legislative power be left unrestrained as it was in England. . . .

All of the unique features of our Constitution show an underlying purpose to create a new kind of limited government. Central to all of the Framers of the Bill of Rights was the idea that since government, particularly the national government newly created, is a powerful institution, its officials—all of them—must be compelled to exercise their powers within strictly defined boundaries. As Madison told Congress, the Bill of Rights' limitations point, "sometimes against the abuse of the Executive power, sometimes against the Legislative, and in some cases against the community itself; or, in other words, against the majority in favor of the minority." Madison also explained that his proposed amendments were intended "to limit and qualify the powers of Government, by excepting out of the grant of power those cases in which the Government ought not to act, or to act only in a particular mode.". . .

Reasons for the Adoption of the Bill of Rights

The Framers were well aware that the individual rights they sought to protect might be easily nullified if subordinated to the general powers granted to Congress. One of the reasons for adoption of the Bill of Rights was to prevent just that. Specifically the people feared that the "necessary and proper" clause could be used to project the generally granted Congressional powers into the protected areas of individual rights. One need only read the debates in the various states to find out that this is true. But if these debates leave any doubt, Mr. Madison's words to Congress should remove it. In speaking of the "necessary and proper" clause and its possible effect on freedom of religion he said, as reported in the Annals of Congress:

> Whether the words are necessary or not, he did not mean to say, but they had been required by some of the State Conventions, who seemed to entertain an opinion that under the clause of the Constitution, which

gave power to Congress to make all laws necessary and proper to carry into execution the Constitution, and the laws made under it, enabled them to make laws of such a nature as might infringe the rights of conscience, and establish a national religion; to prevent these effects he presumed the amendment was intended, and he thought it as well expressed as the nature of the language would admit. . . .

Protection Afforded by the Bill of Rights

Mr. Madison made a clear explanation to Congress that it was the purpose of the First Amendment to grant greater protection than England afforded its citizens. He said:

> In the declaration of rights which that country has established, the truth is, they have gone no farther than to raise a barrier against the power of the Crown; the power of the Legislature is left altogether indefinite. Although I know whenever the great rights, the trial by jury, freedom of the press, or liberty of conscience, come in question in that body, the invasion of them is resisted by able advocates, yet their Magna Charta does not contain any one provision for the security of those rights, respecting which the people of America are most alarmed. The freedom of the press and rights of conscience, those choicest privileges of the people, are unguarded in the British Constitution. . . .

It was the desire to give the people of America greater protection against the powerful Federal Government than the English had had against their government that caused the Framers to put these freedoms of expression, again in the words of Madison, "beyond the reach of this Government.". . .

Of course the decision to provide a constitutional safeguard for a particular right, such as the fair trial requirements of the Fifth and Sixth Amendments and the right of free speech protection of the First, involves a balancing of conflicting interests. Strict procedures may release guilty men; protecting speech and press may involve dangers to a particular government. I believe, however, that the Framers themselves did this balancing when they wrote the Constitution and the Bill of Rights. They appreciated the risks involved and they decided that certain rights should be guaranteed regardless of these risks. Courts have neither the right nor the power to review this original decision of the Framers and to attempt to make a different evaluation of the importance of the rights granted in the Constitution. Where conflicting values exist in the field of individual liberties protected by the Constitution, that document settles the conflict, and its policy should not be changed without constitutional amendments by the people in the manner provided by the people.

Our First Amendment was a bold effort . . . to establish a country with no legal restrictions of any kind upon the subjects people could investigate, discuss and deny.

Misuse of government power, particularly in times of stress, has brought suffering to humanity in all ages about which we have authentic history. Some of the world's noblest and finest men have suffered ignominy and death for no crime—unless unorthodoxy is a crime. Even enlightened Athens had its victims such as Socrates. Because of the same kind of bigotry, Jesus, the great Dissenter, was put to death on a wooden cross. The flames of inquisitions all over the world have warned that men endowed with unlimited government power, even earnest men, consecrated to a cause, are dangerous.

Value of the Bill of Rights Today

For my own part, I believe that our Constitution, with its absolute guarantees of individual rights, is the best hope for the aspirations of freedom which men share everywhere. I cannot agree with those who think of the Bill of Rights as an 18th Century straitjacket, unsuited for this age. It is old but not all old things are bad. The evils it guards against are not only old, they are with us now, they exist today. Almost any morning you open your daily paper you can see where some person somewhere in the world is on trial or has just been convicted of supposed disloyalty to a new group controlling the government which has set out to purge its suspected enemies and all those who had dared to be against its successful march to power. Nearly always you see that these political heretics are being tried by military tribunals or some other summary and sure method for disposition of the accused. Now and then we even see the convicted victims as they march to their execution.

Experience all over the world has demonstrated, I fear, that the distance between a stable, orderly government and one that has been taken over by force is not so great as we have assumed. Our own free system to live and progress has to have intelligent citizens, citizens who cannot only think and speak and write to influence people, but citizens who are free to do that without fear of governmental censorship or reprisal.

A Sacred Trust Between the Government and the People

The provisions of the Bill of Rights that safeguard fair legal procedures came about largely to protect the weak and the oppressed from punishment by the strong and the powerful who wanted to stifle the voices of discontent raised in protest against oppression and injustice in public affairs. Nothing that I have read in the Congressional debates on the Bill of Rights indicates that there was any belief that the First Amendment contained any qualifications. The only arguments that tended to look in this direction at all were those that said "that all paper barriers against the power of the community are too weak to be worthy of attention." Suggestions were also made in and out of Congress that a Bill of Rights would be a futile gesture since there would be no way to enforce the safeguards for freedom it provided. Mr. Madison answered this argument in these words:

> If they [the Bill of Rights amendments] are incorporated into the Constitution, independent tribunals of justice will consider themselves in a peculiar manner the guardians of those rights; they will be an impenetrable bulwark against any assumption of power in the Legislative or Executive; they will be naturally led to resist every encroachment upon rights expressly stipulated for in the Constitution by the declaration of rights.

> I fail to see how courts can escape this sacred trust. Since the earliest days philosophers have dreamed of a

country where the mind and spirit of man would be free; where there would be no limits to inquiry; where men would be free to explore the unknown and to challenge the most deeply rooted beliefs and principles. Our First Amendment was a bold effort to adopt this principle—to establish a country with no legal restrictions of any kind upon the subjects people could investigate, discuss and deny. The Framers knew, better perhaps than we do today, the risks they were taking. They knew that free speech might be the friend of change and revolution. But they also knew that it is always the deadliest enemy of tyranny. With this knowledge they still believed that the ultimate happiness and security of a nation lies in its ability to explore, to change, to grow and ceaselessly to adapt itself to new knowledge born of inquiry free from any kind of governmental control over the mind and spirit of man. Loyalty comes from love of good government, not fear of a bad one.

The First Amendment is truly the heart of the Bill of Rights. The Framers balanced its freedoms of religion, speech, press, assembly and petition against the needs of a powerful central government, and decided that in those freedoms lies this nation's only true security. They were not afraid for men to be free. We should not be. We should be as confident as Jefferson was when he said in his First Inaugural Address:

> If there be any among us who would wish to dissolve this Union or to change its republican form, let them stand undisturbed as monuments of the safety with which error of opinion may be tolerated where reason is left free to combat it.

Appendix: The Bill of Rights in Its Original Language

Amendment 1
Congress shall make no law respecting an establishment of religion, or prohibiting the free exercise thereof; or abridging the freedom of speech, or of the press; or the right of the people peaceably to assemble, and to petition the government for a redress of grievances.

Amendment 2
A well-regulated militia, being necessary to the security of a free state, the right of the people to keep and bear arms shall not be infringed.

Amendment 3
No soldier shall, in time of peace, be quartered in any house, without the consent of the owner, nor in time of war, but in a manner to be prescribed by law.

Amendment 4
The right of the people to be secure in their persons, houses, papers, and effects, against unreasonable searches and seizures, shall not be violated, and no warrants shall issue, but upon probable cause, supported by oath or affirmation, and particularly describing the place to be searched, and the persons or things to be seized.

Amendment 5
No person shall be held to answer for a capital or otherwise infamous crime, unless on the presentment or indictment of a grand jury, except in cases arising in the land or naval forces, or in the militia, when in actual service in time of war or public danger; nor shall any person be subject for the

same offense to be twice put in jeopardy of life or limb; nor shall be compelled in any criminal case to be a witness against himself, nor be deprived of life, liberty, or property, without due process of law; nor shall private property be taken for public use, without just compensation.

Amendment 6

In all criminal prosecutions, the accused shall enjoy the right to a speedy and public trial, by an impartial jury of the state and district wherein the crime shall have been committed, which district shall have been previously ascertained by law, and to be informed of the nature and cause of the accusation; to be confronted with the witnesses against him; to have compulsory process for obtaining witnesses in his favor, and to have the assistance of counsel for defense.

Amendment 7

In suits at common law where the value in controversy shall exceed twenty dollars, the right of trial by jury, shall be preserved, and no fact tried by a jury shall be otherwise reexamined in any court of the United States, than according to the rules of the common law.

Amendment 8

Excessive bail shall not be required, nor excessive fines imposed, nor cruel and unusual punishments inflicted.

Amendment 9

The enumeration in the Constitution, of certain rights, shall not be construed to deny or disparage others retained by the people.

Amendment 10

The powers not delegated to the United States by the Constitution, nor prohibited by it to the states, are reserved to the states respectively, or to the people.

Chronology

1215
English barons force the king to sign the Magna Carta, which legally limits the king's power and establishes the principal of due process.

1628
In England the Petition of Right is passed, establishing the idea that the rule of law is supreme in the land.

1689
The Glorious Revolution occurs in England; it results in a bill of rights that grants liberties in various areas to the people; John Locke publishes his *Second Treatise of Civil Government*, which promotes the idea that government is part of a compact between the governed and the rulers in which the government's job is to secure the natural rights of its citizens.

1765
The Stamp Act Congress calls for key liberties for American colonists.

1776
Virginia adopts a bill of rights, a first for a state; Thomas Jefferson writes the Declaration of Independence, which states that governments derive their power from the consent of the governed.

1781
The Articles of Confederation are adopted without any reference to freedoms because it is assumed that the states would be the ones to grant these to the people.

May 14, 1787
The Constitutional Convention opens.

September 12, 1787
George Mason and Elbridge Gerry ask for a bill of rights, but the delegates vote it down.

September 15, 1787
The Constitution is approved.

September 17, 1787
The Constitution is signed.

December 7, 1787
Delaware becomes the first state to ratify the Constitution; Thomas Jefferson and James Madison begin exchanging letters debating the necessity of a bill of rights; "Brutus" writes a series of anti-Federalist essays that are published over a period of several months while John Jay, James Madison, and Alexander Hamilton begin publishing the *Federalist* papers, which defend the Constitution under debate in the various states; the first federal bill of rights is included in the Northwest Ordinance; it guarantees freedom of religion, the right to trial by jury, habeas corpus, reasonable bail, and bans cruel and unusual punishment.

June 21, 1788
New Hampshire becomes the ninth state to ratify the Constitution, thereby making it the law of the land.

July 2, 1788
The president of Congress announces that the Constitution has been ratified by the necessary nine states; Alexander Hamilton writes *Federalist #84*, which argues against the need for a bill of rights to be part of the Constitution; Patrick Henry and Edmund Randolph debate the need for a bill of rights during Virginia's ratification convention.

1789
James Madison introduces a bill of rights to Congress; Congress submits the first twelve amendments to the states for ratification; New Jersey is the first state to ratify ten of the twelve amendments.

1791
The Bill of Rights, in the form of the first ten amendments to the Constitution, is ratified.

1833
In *Barron v. Baltimore* the Supreme Court rules that the Bill of Rights does not apply to state governments.

1866

Congress sends the Fourteenth Amendment to the states for ratification.

1868

The Fourteenth Amendment is ratified by twenty-eight states and becomes part of the Constitution.

1897

In the *Chicago, Burlington, & Quincy Railroad Company v. Chicago* case, the Supreme Court rules that a clause in the Bill of Rights applies to the state governments because of the due process clause of the Fourteenth Amendment.

1914

The Supreme Court formulates the exclusionary rule, providing that evidence collected by the government in violation of the Fourth Amendment's protection against unlawful search and seizure is inadmissible in a federal court; state courts are unaffected *(Weeks v. United States)*.

1925

In *Gitlow v. New York* the Supreme Court lets stand the conviction of Benjamin Gitlow, a founding member of the American Communist Party, finding that his revolutionary pamphlet *The Left-Wing Manifesto* is not constitutionally protected speech; but the court goes on to rule that freedom of speech and the press are among those personal rights protected by the due process clause of the Fourteenth Amendment, thereby incorporating the First Amendment into the due process clause.

1942

The civil rights of thousands of Japanese Americans are violated as they are placed in internment camps following Japan's attack on Pearl Harbor, the event that signaled U.S. entry into World War II.

1943

The Supreme Court rules that a requirement to salute the flag is a violation of the free speech provision of the First Amendment *(West Virginia State Board of Education v. Barnette)*.

1954

In *Brown v. Board of Education* the Supreme Court rules that a segregated school system is a violation of equal protection.

1961

The Supreme Court incorporates the Fourth Amendment into the due process clause of the Fourteenth Amendment in ruling that evidence seized in violation of the Fourth Amendment cannot be used against a suspect *(Mapp v. Ohio)*.

1963

In *Gideon v. Wainwright*, the Supreme Court rules that an indigent defendant has a right to counsel.

1964

The Supreme Court overturns a libel suit against the *New York Times*, holding that under the First Amendment, debate on public issues should be "uninhibited, robust, and wide open" *(New York Times v. Sullivan)*.

1966

The Supreme Court rules in *Miranda v. Arizona* that a suspect in custody not only has a right to counsel but also a right not to be self-incriminating.

1969

The Supreme Court upholds the right of a student to wear a black armband in protest against the war in Vietnam *(Tinker v. Des Moines Independent School District)*.

1973

The Supreme Court extends the right of privacy to include a woman's right to have an abortion under protection of the Fourteenth Amendment *(Roe v. Wade)*.

1989

In *Texas v. Johnson* the Supreme Court rules that burning the American flag is a form of symbolic speech protected by the First Amendment.

1989–1991

Observance of the bicentennial of the debate over and ratification of the Bill of Rights is marked by national debate about civil liberties in a free society.

For Further Research

Mortimer Adler, *We Hold These Truths*. New York: Macmillan, 1987.

Bernard Bailyn, ed., *The Debate on the Constitution*. New York: Library of America, 1993.

Fred Barbash, *The Founding: A Dramatic Account of the Writing of the Constitution*. New York: Simon & Schuster, 1987.

Richard B. Bernstein, *Are We to Be a Nation?* Cambridge, MA: Harvard University Press, 1987.

Richard B. Bernstein and Jerome Agel, *Amending America*. New York: Times Books, 1993.

Catherine Drinker Bowen, *Miracle at Philadelphia*. Boston: Atlantic Monthly, 1986.

Irving Brant, *The Bill of Rights*. Indianapolis: Bobbs-Merrill, 1965.

George W. Carey, *The Federalist*. Chicago: University of Illinois Press, 1994.

William Dudley, ed., *Opposing Viewpoints: The Bill of Rights*. San Diego: Greenhaven, 1994.

———, *Opposing Viewpoints: The Creation of the Constitution*. San Diego: Greenhaven, 1995.

Doris Faber and Harold Faber, *We the People*. New York: Charles Scribner's Sons, 1987.

Ira Glasser, *Visions of Liberty*. New York: Arcade, 1991.

Claude Heathcock, *The United States Constitution in Perspective*. Boston: Allyn and Bacon, 1968.

Michael Kammen, *A Machine That Would Go of Itself: The Constitution in American Culture*. New York: Alfred A. Knopf, 1986.

Michael Kammen, ed., *The Origins of the American Constitution*. New York: Penguin Books, 1986.

Philip A. Klinkner, *The American Heritage History of the Bill of Rights: The First Amendment*. Englewood Cliffs, NJ: Silver Burdett, 1991.

Forrest McDonald, *Novus Ordo Seclorum: The Intellectual Origins of the Constitution*. Lawrence: University of Kansas Press, 1985.

Charles L. Mee Jr., *The Genius of the People*. New York: Harper and Row, 1987.

Saul K. Padover and Jacob W. Landynski, *The Living U.S. Constitution*. New York: New American Library, 1983.

William Peters, *A More Perfect Union: The Men and Events That Made the Constitution*. New York: Crown, 1987.

J.R. Pole, ed., *The American Constitution—For and Against*. New York: Hill & Wang, 1987.

Jack N. Rakove, *Original Meanings*. New York: Alfred A. Knopf, 1997.

Clinton Rossiter, *1787: The Grand Convention*. New York: Macmillan, 1966.

Robert Rutland, *The Ordeal of the Constitution: The Antifederalists and the Ratification Struggle of 1787–1788*. Boston: Northeastern University Press, 1983.

Index